D0538006

HELIGAN

Fruit, Flowers and Herbs

9112000064476

HELIGAN

Fruit, Flowers and Herbs

Philip McMillan Browse

Alison Hodge

BRENT LIBRARIES	
KIL	
91120000064476	
Askews & Holts	15-Aug-2012
635.0942	£14.95

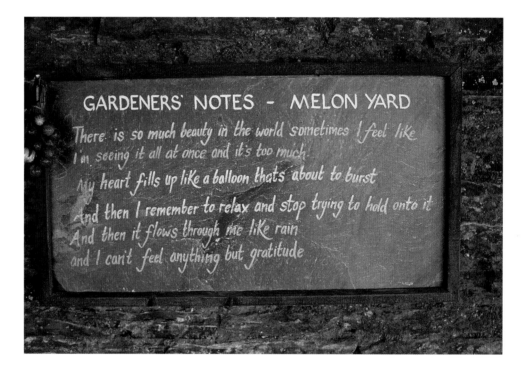

The Lost Gardens of Heligan are open daily all year round.
For further information please visit www.heligan.com, or contact:
The Lost Gardens of Heligan, Pentewan, St Austell, Cornwall PL26 6EN,
tel: 01726 845100; fax: 01726 845101; email: info@heligan.com

CONTENTS

FOREWORD

PETER THODAY

Heligan is rightly world famous as a restored late nineteenth-century garden that has become one of the country's most popular visitor attractions. Remarkably it has managed to please three very different audiences: the hundreds of thousands looking for a day out in beautiful rural surroundings; the tens of thousands of knowledgeable amateur gardeners, and that potentially most hard to please group, the professional horticulturists and garden designers.

Much of this success comes from Heligan's willingness to share with its visitors its enthusiasm and the challenges it has faced. There can be no better example of this than its struggle to grow a wide range of fruits and flowers in the climate of central Cornwall. The great private gardens of Britain were not located for the convenience of their gardeners, struggling to meet the expectations of the big house. They were adjuncts to the country mansions located on family estates scattered across the length and breadth of Britain, often far removed from 'an ideal place to garden'.

Heligan has never shirked the challenge to emulate these efforts. Of course, by Heligan I mean the people who run the place and, in true Heligan style this includes everyone, from Peter Stafford, the Managing Director to the humblest in the workforce. Right at the centre of that pack of enthusiasts sits, or more accurately, walks about, that arch stickler for horticultural correctness, Philip McMillan Browse. From the outset he has been central to Heligan's horticultural credibility, and as the garden staff will testify he has always been on hand advising, directing, encouraging but never compromising in the ambition to make these once lost gardens relive their past.

The Lost Gardens of Heligan were lucky: they were found at just the right time – not that I think the timing would have made any difference to Tim Smit, he surely would have done his own thing regardless of fashion. Nevertheless, it certainly helped that people were starting to wonder about the craft of cultivation as well as enjoying the beauty and grandeur of well-maintained pleasure grounds. Increasing numbers of visitors to our great country gardens were starting to question what had gone on within the high-walled enclosures in which they were now asked to park their cars. The same kind of people were looking beyond the beautiful grading and packing of the fruit and vegetables on offer in the shops, and thinking that they would rather swap these for a bit more variety and freshness. A combination of these seemingly unrelated ideas, together with the very longstanding love of seeing things in the making, gave the Heligan gang fertile ground upon which to wow the visitors as month by month and year by year the restoration progressed. Picking a date, or rather a period, for the restoration was easy as the garden was known to have been at its peak in the closing years of the nineteenth century, and in near terminal decline as a result of the First World War. So the reborn Heligan became a prime example of a late Victorian country house grounds with, at its heart, a complex of productive walled gardens. It is, of course, in these productive walled gardens and their glasshouses that the fruits and flowers described in this book flourish alongside the vegetables already covered in *The Heligan Vegetable Bible*.

The restoration was so successful and so fast that it seemed that such crops and their cultural methods could be conjured up from nowhere. Nothing could be further from the truth. It would have been impossible to have put together this extremely complex living horticultural reconstruction without a team of people pooling their various skills, from John Nelson's massive and diverse mastery of the building trade's crafts to Philip's understanding of plant cultivation. People look in vain for 'the old gardener' in the team; there was no such person! Indeed, I have no doubt that the project gained from his absence. Far better that the challenges were analysed by Philip McMillan Browse. Philip used his scientific training to see through and solve problems, often anticipating their appearance. He then produced some of the most accurate period-correct husbandry programmes ever contrived. I often wonder about the synergistic effect of Philip and Tim working together in the early days of the restoration. Tim's first training was in archaeology, and Philip set up what stands year on year as a piece of horticultural experimental archaeology; not, I think planned but perhaps subliminal empathy.

All this focus on the late Victorian period's productive walled gardens, both at Heligan and elsewhere, celebrates the last great flowering of the craft of what I call 'handmade crops'. But there is a danger in this focus: it obscures the history upon which this zenith was built. We can marvel at the cunning with which the gardener of 100 years ago used bell cloches or heated his pineapple pit or grafted then trained his apple trees without realizing where and when such skills arrived in the British walled garden. That's another book. But I can tell you that it should start with the words 'Far away and long ago', although it's not a fairy story!

Finally, I welcome another Heligan book. As with the others the style informs and entertains, but once again, woven within the text, and of great long-term value, are the results of this extraordinary experiment in garden archaeology.

INTRODUCTION

CANDY SMIT

Philip needs no introduction in the world of horticulture; but perhaps this, his latest book, does; for he is so self-effacing that in reading it you might not otherwise appreciate the true extent of his contribution to Heligan. The present-day Flower Garden here is one of my favourite places on this earth and of all the people I have met, Philip is one of the most unusual. The one was created by the other. I have been privileged to witness this process and along the way to acquire a mentor and a special friend.

I remember during the early days of clearance at Heligan, in 1990 and 1991, that Tim would come home and tell me about the occasional visits of the Cornwall County Horticultural Advisor from Probus Demonstration Garden, who came to give advice on which specimens to save from the rampant tangle of boughs and thorns – which in those days spread pretty much across the whole site, well above head height. This gent was a somewhat stiff, well-read, correctly dressed, middle-aged scientist, to all intents and purposes completely out of place in the surrounding chaos. But I think he enjoyed his trips out to Heligan, witnessing the adventure of amateur restoration unfurl on an enormous scale; the almost unprecedented gamble driven by those unlikely bedfellows, Tim Smit and John Nelson. The standing joke was that Tim did all the talking and John did all the work; but in the end it was Philip who realized the potential of the horticultural opportunity they both created.

Tim's introduction to Heligan was in the company of John Willis, who had recently come of the age to take responsibility for this, part of his local Tremayne inheritance. Tim's first sight was of a densely overgrown and decaying wreck and he was inspired, not as a gardener but as an archaeologist, to uncover what had happened here. Who? When? How? Why? His interest was in past people, not so much precious plants *per se*; but in the human capacity for achievement, whether it be horticultural or anything else. Never less than determined (and with an already firmly established reputation among friends and family for being driven by wild and unrealistic ideas), Tim spent the following five years single-mindedly summoning the resources necessary to put the life back into (as he coined it) 'The Lost Gardens of Heligan'.

The derelict Paxton House in the Flower Garden, after initial clearance, 1993

Labour and materials… John Nelson's physical and mental stamina proved close to super-human, while Tim's gift of the gab won countless free loans of equipment during a period of severe recession and secured Heligan's name on the airwaves. But it was Philip's knowledge – and infectious quest for it – that gave the project the meat that has ensured its enduring respect. He was soon tempted to join the team, and gradually constructed plans to re-create a

Tim Smit and John Nelson face a TV crew in the derelict Flower Garden, 1993 (top)
The same camera angle 18 months later (above)

Victorian kitchen garden within the areas at Heligan originally designated 'productive' – i.e. to restore horticultural structures to function, by reintroducing traditional varieties, grown by traditional methods.

It was Philip's academic tenacity and strength of personality that also empowered the rest of the team to restore the gardens to full function. Our almost unquestioning respect resulted in him securing pretty much a free rein in the productive areas. He insisted on clearing the whole site and starting again completely. There were some tense and tearful moments when we tried to negotiate the saving of three old apple trees and some beautiful self-seeded willows; but he would not be swayed by sentiment. Growing conditions for productive crops had to be right.

Over the past ten years, since 1994 when the first new fruit trees went into the Melon Yard, he has been a tutor for a succession of teams in the modern-day productive gardens at Heligan. The re-establishment of daily/weekly/seasonal/annual horticultural activity here is our living tribute to the men who

Mostly annual crops fill this bare ground, year on year

Terracotta forcing pots for rhubarb and seakale in the Vegetable Garden: in Winter (top), and Spring (above)

went before – and departed for the Great War. Philip is responsible for masterminding this. In return for their implementing his vision, the productive gardens staff have benefited from Philip's fundamental desire to pass on his knowledge and keep these valuable horticultural traditions alive into the future.

The restoration at Heligan has had the benefit of very little horticultural archive. Much was lost in a fire half-way through the twentieth century, and very little record-keeping was ever undertaken anyway in productive areas, save the workbooks (right, dating from 1915) and accounts. Skills were handed down through the generations and seldom described for others on paper.

Philip's research was mostly into productive plants of the Victorian period, and into sourcing relevant stock. In 1999 he compiled his first volume on Heligan crops, *The Heligan Vegetable Bible*, and since then he and I have been plotting the sequel, *Heligan: Fruit, Flowers and Herbs*. The two together provide a comprehensive summary of what is grown in the productive gardens at Heligan today. Our hope is that what is published here will be considered an authoritative archive representing Heligan at the turn of the twentieth century, a hundred years after its original hey-day. These are not simply reference books, but records of what has been grown and how, in a place to which we are both devoted.

I love to watch the productive gardens change through the seasons: the monochromes and great emptiness of enclosed geometric spaces, which become more clearly defined as they descend into Winter; the devotion of many man-months of hard labour to nourish these skeletal areas; the birth of a new season and the exciting step-by-step redecoration of these brilliantly designed gardens – which ascends to an annual peak of production, as the colour and scent literally rise up out of the ground towards you and a summer breeze ripples along the rows of flowers, disturbing the butterflies and the bees.

This is all an extraordinarily sensual experience – and that without even mentioning the mood of the climate or the age of the day. Pass through the great green door beside the Vinery on a bright, new May morning and feel the heat of the sun already building against the mellow brick walls; catch the scent of the wallflowers in their little triangular beds, protected by immaculate box

Sunflower whimsy (top)
Helenium 'Riverton Beauty' (above)

hedges – which I remember being set out from scratch into the vacant acreage less than a decade ago; spot the rows of mesmerizing blue camassia as they sparkle beneath the pink clouds of ancient rhododendrons, billowing over the wall from Sikkim. Even in the springtime, it can all simply be too much.

As for Summer, I relish the occasional chance I get to wander along the walls of sweet peas, soaking up the sun myself in the same way the flowers do... the experience of everything flourishing, in the peak of health – and happiness. There is a tremendous sense in the Flower Garden at this time of year, that our visitors have arrived in a place they want to be; that they suddenly recall something basic and joyous from their past; they gasp, they stand and stare, they sit and dream. They watch us gathering flowers into bunches, armfuls, buckets (nay, barrows), as though such a simple pleasure had been banned from their existence. Sowing, growing and harvesting are fundamental processes on this planet, and yet most of us have been removed from them (unwittingly). Deprived of the opportunity to be involved, and hence to understand, we can so easily ignore nature's essential patterns, rhythm and pace.

Philip says the sweet peas are typically cleared after August bank holiday. Where would a gardener be without a diary, the gradually ingrained schedules that become second nature the longer you stay? There is a tremendous sense of sadness as the curtain of fading colour is rolled away for another year; but then there are the golden joys of Autumn in those dewy mornings, the lovely bronze heleniums, the rudbeckia, the ever-reliable chrysanths. The helichrysum is cut and tied and hung to dry, and the harvest routines kick in. There is a creeping sense of continual motion and certainty, rise and fall, joy and sadness, hope and loss.

Philip himself admits to having no aesthetic sense, although his interests are broad and he is a supporter of the arts. When he plans what is to be grown, he considers all the elements of good horticulture and one gets the sense that in his endeavour to replicate Victorian exactitude he has found his ultimate satisfaction. He loves to work with people who want to learn and he insists on mathematical precision and scientific good practice. However, the uncanny thing is that in sustaining this purely productive approach he has created tracts of unsurpassed, if passing, beauty.

With the passage of time he has become more tolerant of what he terms 'whimsy'. Latterly he has permitted the indulgences of his staff, whether it be Johanna with her morning glory, Helen with her sunflowers or Kathy with her messages acknowledging Peter Rabbit. His description of his own desire to house the gorgeous *Hardenbergia* in the Peach House for the simple reason that its stunning purple haze is a harbinger of the season to come evidences that the hard man has a heart.

Although not a Cornishman, Philip has a strong attachment to the far South-west. He spent some of his childhood on the Isles of Scilly, while his father was headmaster on St Mary's. Clearly his memories of this time are a constant reference for him. Since the structure of the Flower Garden was restored, in 1994, he has striven to succeed with gladioli, traditionally a favoured crop on the Scillies. Year

on year we have endeavoured to deter him, as the rows where the bulbs have been planted remained steadfastly, almost embarrassingly barren. It seems fitting that this book should finally go to print, after their first really successful season on site. The gladioli in 2004 were tremendous – and sentiment is vindicated.

The productive garden is a fragile creation, born largely of routine annual activity, tremendous focus and human

perseverance. Without the continual input of experienced labour, day in, day out, it would soon disappear in an ocean of weeds, as those at Heligan did before. There is a real sense that these special moments in time we enjoy here now, in Spring, Summer, Autumn or Winter, are achieved by sustaining a perfect balance in the relationship between man and nature.

This requires both wisdom and sensitivity. Underneath it all, Philip has them both.

The Dipping Pool (top), and the Head Gardener's Office in Winter (above); autumn produce in the Potting Shed (left)

CHAPTER 1
THE STAGE

Heligan House was the principal residence of the Tremayne family until the First World War. A large, imposing building with views over Mevagissey to the sea, it was at the heart of a significant estate (right) that had held a dominant position in the area for some 300 years. The First World War saw the beginnings of its demise as the home of the family, and despite the best attentions of tenants during the inter-war years and after the Second World War, the house and gardens gradually declined. The house was sold off in 1970 and converted into apartments, and eventually most of the surrounding buildings were also converted into residential accommodation. Meanwhile, the gardens, apart from those immediately around the house, gradually became overgrown and fell into disrepair. In the mild Cornish climate, with its year-round growth pattern, it does not take long for a garden to be almost completely lost – 25 years is plenty of time for ash and sycamore to reach a majestic size on any reasonable soil, and the growth of brambles, pheasant berry and willow has to be seen to be appreciated. The story of the early days of the resurrection of the gardens is well chronicled in *The Lost Gardens of Heligan*, a book which reflects the vision and resolve of Tim Smit and the many other people who contributed to the initial salvage work. It has been the members of that team and those immediately following who have, over the course of the decade after the first clearances, contributed to what is now a thriving garden, visitor attraction and business.

Since the period in which the initial clearances were undertaken, the various elements of the gardens have been uncovered and identified: the pleasure grounds, the several small 'private' gardens, the Jungle, the productive gardens and, more recently, the extended estate and the woodlands have all had their share of attention. More distant areas, such as Temple Wood, are still to receive attention. These various areas are all significant parts of what was originally a harmonious whole. Within the context of a nineteenth-century estate, however, the principal features would have been the farm and the productive gardens, as they were the life-blood of its existence, providing the food and materials needed to maintain the whole enterprise. The productive gardens (centre right) were principally a facility to provide sufficient vegetables, fruit, flowers and herbs to service the expectations of the big house. They were a necessity, not a luxury, although that

The heart of the gardens restored: below Heligan House lie the
Walled (Flower) Garden, the Melon Yard and the Vegetable Garden

Heligan House at the end of the twentieth century

is not to say that they did not produce luxury crops as more sophisticated cultivation techniques and sufficient financial resources became available. The relevant aspects of vegetable gardening have been outlined in *The Heligan Vegetable Bible*. The present volume is intended to be a companion, and deals with the flowers, fruit and herbs grown in these productive gardens.

THE PRODUCTIVE GARDENS

Heligan's productive gardens consist of a Vegetable Garden; a small, early, walled garden (the Melon Yard) dating from the early part of the eighteenth century and containing a later greenhouse, Pineapple Pit and frames; a more conventional, brick-built early nineteenth-century Walled Garden of approximately half an acre, but of eccentric ground-plan and containing lean-to greenhouses; a Reserve Garden, which is a side room to the Walled Garden, and ancillary buildings and orchards.

The productive gardens at Heligan are not very typical of the usual run of such operations, and are not nearly as complex as gardens further north, as they were designed to take into account the influence of those elements which are peculiar to this Cornish site. The first of these influences is the mildness of the climate, and Heligan therefore has relatively few glasshouses. It was anticipated that the variety of production could be achieved either with the use of cold frames or hotbeds, or even out-of-doors. However, in Cornwall the ever-present disadvantage is the wind, which often develops considerable force. Normally the wind is fairly benign, insofar as it arrives from the South-west, is mild, and usually of low velocity; but it can reach frightening speeds and forces which cause massive damage, particularly when it comes from the North or East. In the Winter and Spring the north and east winds bring very low temperatures, so all Cornish gardens need to establish effective shelter. The main productive gardens at Heligan are sited for maximum advantage, with a north-south axis on a gentle, south-facing slope, each segment one below the other on rising ground to the north of the house. They had considerable defences against the wind from all angles, bar due south.

At the top (northerly) end of this sequence is the **Vegetable Garden** (above). Approximately one and a quarter acres in area, it has an unusual shape, with the north-east (right) and north-west corners of the rectangle splayed out to give areas where the sun concentrates either in the morning or the evening. The site

is protected on the northern boundary with an evergreen conifer hedge of western red cedar (*Thuja plicata*), and on the eastern and western sides by hedges of cherry laurel (*Prunus laurocerasus*). All the hedges are maintained at eight feet tall. The southern boundary is provided by the curved wall of the contiguous Melon Yard, the earlier and smaller of the walled gardens.

The replanting of the northern hedge provides an example of the processes which were involved in many of the decisions guiding the restoration of the gardens in the early years. After the clearance of the area, the original line of the hedge was indicated by several 30ft.-high Lawson's cypress trees in a straight line (below). Further investigation revealed a broken granite threshold stone in this line, which showed the position of the gate. In the initial clearances, these now valueless trees were removed. Logic dictated that we should replant with the same species, but at this time (1993) there had appeared in Cornwall several outbreaks of *Corynebacterium* canker in cypress hedges, and as we had no wish to replant something that might succumb to the disease, we chose to use the Western red cedar, as it was not susceptible and was 'period correct'. We planted the young trees at seven-foot intervals. This was the sort of spacing that might have been used in the Victorian period and also reflected, to a certain extent, the number of matching trees we were able to obtain! The making of immediate full cover was not an essential feature to the Victorians: they were quite prepared to wait for good quality shelter.

Northern entrance to the Vegetable Garden, 1992

The chief purpose of the Vegetable Garden is to provide the main site for the production of the staple vegetable crops. It also contains the soft fruit, strawberry and rhubarb crops and, on the back wall of the Melon Yard, fruit bushes and trees are trained. A fair amount of cut-flower crops are also interspersed with the vegetables, where space permits and the flowers are compatible with the vegetables' cropping programme. The garden is divided by an off-centre, north-south path, aligned with the doors into the Melon Yard, and a cross path is set half way down the garden. The main path is decorated with apple trees, planted at ten-foot intervals, which have been trained to grow in an arch. Such a fruit arch was a common feature in a kitchen garden as it provided an interesting and decorative walk for the proprietor and his guests as they perambulated through to other areas. Normally the trees on this arch would have been pears, but we have

The newly planted Thuja hedge, 1993, in place of the huge cypresses (opposite)

used apples due to the high local incidence of canker, a disease that thrives in the mild, damp Cornish climate, and to which most suitable pears are highly susceptible. The path has also been lined with a low box hedge, behind which are beds of flowers to provide additional colour and interest (see next pages). All of this ground-plan and planting is based on an informed understanding of what might be typical of the era as no plans, planting, or archaeological evidence survived.

Below the Vegetable Garden is the **Melon Yard**, probably the first 'protected area' to have been developed in the gardens. This area is relatively small and represents a chronology of sophistications and enlargements since its establishment in *c.* 1700. The initial part of this structure was the curved, south-facing wall, which is about six to eight feet high and about 100 ft. in length. In the front (i.e. to the south) of this, much milder conditions are created. This wall was built of shillet, principally because it is the local stone, but also because there were no bricks available in Cornwall at the time, due to the lack of suitable clay. However, in about 1720, a small deposit of suitable clay was discovered on the estate, so a kiln was built and bricks were made for a period of about 40 years. By this time the effectiveness of bricks as heat sinks was recognized, and this back wall was raised to about 14 ft., mainly using the shillet, but faced with bricks on its south-

facing aspect – an effective and economical use of the limited supply of bricks. Subsequently the yard was enclosed with shillet walls, and various vernacular buildings were also built in. Most of the suitable walls were then covered with fruit trees and vines.

It would appear that at or before the turn of the eighteenth century the Pineapple Pit had been established in its earliest incarnation. Subsequently it evolved to the design which is now extant and restored, and which probably dates from *c.* 1820. During the middle of the nineteenth century, the yard was laid out with various permanent frames covered with English lights (six-foot by four-foot glass frames). Although these structures look as though they are made of modern concrete blocks, they are in fact nineteenth-century and are constructed of blocks made of Roman Cement, which would have been cast on site. Soon afterwards, the present Melon House was erected, together with its boiler and boiler housing. This house is designed as a 5/8 'hip' house, oriented East-West – as indeed are all the frames in this garden – in order to make the best use of the winter light. All of the glass in these structures shows the

The Melon Yard: a spring view (above), and 12 years earlier (bottom left); the curved, south-facing wall (left, middle: during and top: after restoration, with the Melon House and Pineapple Pit on the right)

'beaver-tail' cut (right), which was used to prevent the premature rotting of the thin glazing bars that support the narrow runs of glass. The glazing bars were lightweight and thin in order not to exclude too much light, and the glass panes were narrow as at this time they were manufactured by the barrel process. The beaver-tail cut caused rainwater to run down the middle of the glass panes, away from the perishable wood.

During the nineteenth century this yard would have been used principally for the production of out-of-season crops during the Autumn, Winter and Spring. During the early summer months the frames would have been used for the raising of young plants for transplanting, and were then probably cropped with melons

and cucumbers The considerable number of nail-holes in the south- and west-facing walls indicates that they were used for training fruit trees. We have planted fruit trees on the walls again, supported by and tied into tensioned wires, which represent the advance of technology in the later part of the nineteenth century. The dark house, in the bottom of the building that houses the Fruit Room, is used principally for cropping mushrooms, which are installed during the New Year period. Around the gate in the wall which leads into the Vegetable Garden is a decorative pergola which has a rose, 'Felicité et Perpetue', trained on one side, and on the other a Burmese honeysuckle, *Lonicera hildebrandiana*, which has thrived here since 1996. It has no right to survive in this climate, but exemplifies how particularly advantageous microclimatic niches can sometimes be found and exploited.

Adjacent to Heligan House is the most southerly productive area, the larger **Walled Garden**, nowadays often referred to as the Flower Garden. It is unusual for this part of the world in that it is built of bricks. There appears to be no conclusive evidence as to the date of its erection, but the ages of its lean-to greenhouses and the styles of building suggest that it is most likely to have been built no later than 1830. How this facility came to be built of brick is also a matter of conjecture. There is reasonable circumstantial evidence to suppose that the small ships plying between Pentewan and ports in the Low Countries, transporting porcelain-grade china clay, were commissioned by the squire to return with ballasts of brick – the Tremaynes did have interests in this trade. The ground-plan of this Walled Garden is intriguing insofar as it is built around a shallow valley running from North to South, and with the ground sloping up and back from it, giving slopes which face South-south-west (left) and South-south-east respectively. The only right angle in the layout of the walls is in the south-east corner: the south-facing northern wall runs in a direction very slightly to the south of east, and the east wall is angled to face South-south-west at the top of the slope. This orientation gives the very best opportunity to make use of winter sunshine.

This garden also contains a number of simple but interesting glasshouses, all of which are lean-to in design. The oldest of these (derelict, below), dating from *c.* 1830, is now known as the Citrus House and is home to our collection of citrus trees during the Winter. Originally the end walls were built of brick, and only the roof and the front walls contained glass. The superstructure of this house is extremely heavy, with substantial rafters supporting the roof and its sliding vents. It is sited on the south-facing wall and is approximately 14 ft. wide and 28 ft. long. When we were renovating the house, internal excavation prior to the laying of a brick floor revealed that, below ground level, the

front wall was supported on four 4-ft.-high arches (previous page, top), indicating that the building was intended to be a vinery. In such houses it was the practice to prepare a deeply cultivated area in front of the house to allow an extensive root run for the vines. The main south-facing wall was originally built as a heated flue wall, heated by a furnace. The hollow wall acted as a chimney, which was designed to weave backwards and forwards and so deliver hot air all along the wall. Its north-facing side was built as three courses of bricks to provide insulation, and the front side only one course thick to allow the heat to permeate readily.

The Paxton House was probably erected in about 1850, the period during which this type of glasshouse was manufactured and marketed. Its construction is described in Chapter 7. At some time in the second half of the nineteenth century, both the Paxton House and the Citrus House were adapted to be heated by hot water from a coal-fired boiler, delivered through four-inch diameter cast-iron pipes on a gravitational circulation system (excavated remains, above).

The Peach House (top, derelict) is heated naturally, and appears to have been built at some time after 1880, as it is constructed to be glazed with 14-ins.-wide panes of horticultural glass. Its south-south-west orientation and the pitch of its roof are designed to make the most of winter and early spring sunshine. There were obviously other houses here, as can be seen from the marks on the wall and the indications on various maps, but these had already disappeared by the 1890s. Records of the ground-plan of this Walled Garden in its productive heyday do not appear to survive, so the present-day layout is an informed approximation of the nineteenth-century design.

The **Reserve Garden** is contiguous with the Walled Garden and was con-structed as a small side room, to provide a protected area in which plants could be raised for use in the Vegetable and Walled Gardens. It now contains an inter-esting, patented, double-sided, cold frame (above). The cast-iron pieces of this structure were made by Foster & Pearson of Beeston in about 1880 and, although not original to the garden, we obtained it in the very early days of the recovery on the basis that it was an offer that was too good to refuse. The productive gardens also incorporate the **Orchards**. Historically, these have had various sites in the surrounding estate. Our present orchards are between Shepherd's Barn and the Stewardry, where the poultry are kept, and alongside Horsemoor Wood. Their particular interest currently is that they contain a fair selection of local, endemic, West-country varieties.

MANAGING THE PRODUCTIVE GARDENS

The prime motivation for the Head Gardener when managing the productive gardens was, and is, to achieve the best possible and highest quality yields from the crops grown, while maintaining the greatest possible productivity, both in terms of continuous use of the land and of the manpower at his disposal. The

ability to deliver these expectations depended on the development and maintenance of a highly fertile soil and a skilled workforce. High fertility of the soil,
enabling it to support the intensity of production expected, depended on a strict
husbandry regime. This required an understanding of the balance of effects engendered by the requirements of each particular crop, and thus the principles
underlying the need for rotation, manuring and fertilizing; adherence to a rigorous pattern of spacing, thinning and plant manipulation; the proper control of
pests and diseases, and an ability to recognize local weather patterns – all of this
coupled with an innate flexibility which allowed a response to the pattern of each
season as it unfolded, and the changing needs of the House.

The basis of a fertile soil depends principally on the development of a high
proportion of crumb structures in the soil, which in turn is dependent on the
incorporation of large quantities of organic matter. Such material decomposes
continuously until the end product, humus, is attained. Humus is a glue-like
material which bonds the inorganic constituents of the soil into crumb structures
by the activities of the various types of soil fauna and the movements caused by
the pressure of expanding plant roots. It is important to realize that these structures do not withstand physical impacts very well, and consequently the use

of hand operations is a significant
part of the process. If the ability to
manage by hand is not feasible, the
use of equipment that has the least
impact (such as spading machines)
is to be recommended: rotavators
are definitely not appropriate.

The need to incorporate relatively large quantities of organic
matter into the soil means that
a variety of sources have to be
tapped, and these come in several
different guises in the kitchen
garden situation. On average, our
application rates of such material
run to at least 20 tons per acre per
annum. This is the necessary level
required to provide a consistent
reservoir of humus, not only to
create the crumb structures but also
to provide sufficient water-holding
capacity so that the need for water-

ing is reduced to only 'watering in' new plants. The most
significant of our sources, in
terms of quantity, are well-
rotted manure and compost
from green garden waste.
Both of these, when used in
the garden, are already well
on the decomposition path
and are relatively benign, in
that most of the heat from the
decomposition of fresh material has already been dissipat-
ed. Well-rotted manure is the
end product from the practice
of operating a hotbed system.
It is, in effect, fresh stable
manure which has already
had the heat of rapid decomposition withdrawn, that heat
being used to maintain the
temperature in the Pineapple
Pits in our case. Green-waste
compost is made in purpose-
built compost heaps (left),
sited in suitable parts of the

Philip laying seaweed on the first asparagus bed

garden. The heat of the rapid decomposition process, which is encouraged in
the compost heaps, helps to sterilize the material as well as creating a benign
product. With proper management our heaps need about four months to break
down to a useable condition. Each has a raw material capacity of some ten cubic
yards: this reduces to about half of that amount by the time the compost is suitable for incorporation into the soil. Fresh manure from several sources is always
available, but it is best to stack it for a while before using it in the garden to allow
the decomposition process to begin. The chief drawback if it is used in the raw
condition in relatively large and concentrated quantities is that considerable heat
may be generated, which can cause damage to young, fragile root systems and to
tuberous plants such as potatoes, and may also cause 'fanging' of root crops.

   One of the advantages of our maritime location is our ability to collect ('drag')
seaweed and use it as a source of organic matter. Seaweeds are relatively primitive plants, having little in the way of internal structures to decompose, and are

protected from the effects of the saltiness of the seawater by considerable quantities of mucilage, which is already close to humus in composition. Seaweed becomes available during the Autumn after an easterly gale, when large quantities appear on local beaches. We drag it and spread it on any vacant land in the kitchen gardens to a depth of about four inches (above). By the New Year it has reduced to a thin, brittle crust (left) and is easily worked into the soil.

This extended description of soil structures is not meant to appear obsessional; rather, it is based on an understanding of soil fertility as a complex pattern of influences created by the balances and interactions between the chemical, physical and biological influences in the soil, and of soil structures as an integral part of that overall ideal which is fertility. Through their physical effects, these structures play a significant role in holding and buffering soil nutrients: they buffer variations in the pH (acidity/alkalinity) of the soil, improve aeration and water-holding capacity, and also improve drainage and create an environment in which soil creatures are able to flourish in a beneficial ecological balance and so set up suitable physical and chemical balances. All of this sounds like a statement of intent for the extremes of the organic husbandry movement – indeed, there is little to distinguish the greater proportion of these ideals from the outpourings of the 'organic fringe'. What makes our approach different is that, although we wish to create as harmonious a soil environment, in which crops flourish, as is reasonable, we need to be pragmatic. We select our methods on the basis of good practice and adopt an approach best described as sustainable. In effect, we do use chemical pesticides if that is the only way to protect a crop; but this is nevertheless a position of last resort. We are extremely circumspect in the use of such chemicals, both in determining which are used and how often they are applied. Similarly, we are not averse to using some 'artificial' fertilizers if they are relatively pure (as they usually are these days). It was normally the contaminants left from the industrial manufacturing process which caused the problems in the past, and not the compound itself: as a learned friend of mine says, 'As far as the plant is concerned, a nitrogen atom is a nitrogen atom, wherever it has arrived from.'

Paramount to the achievement of success, however, was and is the strict adherence to a basic pattern of operation and rigorous attention to detail. In the context of the nineteenth century, failure to deliver could not be readily rectified, as there was little or no opportunity to make up from elsewhere. Although the Head Gardener would have to be intelligent, capable and experienced, he would nevertheless have had to depend on the skills of the individual gardeners, both in terms of those with specialist interests and those who carried out the basic elements. Gardening is principally about routine and the mundane, with a modicum of interesting tasks thrown in: the satisfaction is, in the end, that of seeing a job well done. Hence, success is as much about the labour force, at all levels, as about any other component.

Philip McMillan Browse with Katharine Cartwright (left) and Johanna Lausen-Higgins

CHAPTER 2

THE CAST

The latter-day recovery of the Lost Gardens of Heligan has, from its inception, been an entrepreneurially based project, surviving on its merits and its ability to attract paying visitors: it has no 'deep pocket' to bail it out in times of need. The project has always been sustained by the vision, enthusiasm, talent and sheer graft of the pioneering spirits in the early years, led by the enthusiasm and personality of Tim Smit. It now builds on this firm base. Apart from the technical aspects of the restoration process, much of that talent was displayed in foreseeing what would interest the public. From very early on it was decided that, because of the interest shown by the earliest visitors to the gardens, the unique selling point of Heligan should be the restoration of its productive gardens. Associated with this is a unique celebration of the lives of those who worked in them – the gardeners and tradesmen, with perhaps only a passing nod to the squirearchy. All of these factors, combined with the character, ambience and photogenic nature of the gardens themselves, would, it was hoped, provide an overall package which would be attractive to visitors.

Time has moved on, and almost inevitably Heligan's philosophy has changed subtly as the project grew. The total area now involved is nearer 200 acres than the original 50-odd, and the development and restoration embraces a concept that is summed up as 'the best of the old and the best of the new'. The project has grown to include the estate, the surrounding farmland and the wildlife, and is not just about pastiche restoration. However, the productive gardens remain as the jewel in the crown – working gardens in which high-quality production is paramount, and where the crops are grown to provide materials for the kitchen and for decoration. The Lost Gardens of Heligan and subsequently the Eden Project, which grew out of Heligan, are both products of their time, when the blend of characters, circumstances and a *raison d'être* all happened to be in place and, most importantly, chimed with the public mood.

An understanding of the value of publicity, and how this is managed effectively in order to gain maximum exposure and achieve the greatest benefit, has been one of Heligan's (and indeed Eden's) triumphs. This is a tribute to Tim's perspicacity. His success in attracting a sound visitor base and wide public following has also provided for the development of a firm financial foundation on

Philip with Gillian Cartwright, admiring the restored Flower Garden in its first Spring

which the business can continue to flourish and develop. Within that successful creation, which has become the Lost Gardens of Heligan, the success of the development of its productive gardens has been a significant contributory, as well as a talismanic, component. This success, however, is as much about the people who make things happen as it is about the plants that provide the show and entertain the visitor – although that is not to say that the staff do not also inform and entertain on occasion! The re-creation of the productive gardens is testimony to the wholehearted effort and support of the entire team. It inevitably reflects the skills, knowledge and talents of particular individuals whose task it is to create and manage the stage on which the play is presented annually – acted out over the seasons with a seamless regularity which alters only marginally as further sophistication of the processes is built into the routine. This special type of gardening really does reflect the year-on-year timelessness of the process which was so familiar to our forebears, whose lives and sacrifice we celebrate. It is this reflection of an old certainty and regularity that so captivates today's visitors.

The present productive garden team is building on the foundations laid by several of their earlier colleagues who made the present-day situation possible. This was achieved by dint of their pioneering work in getting the site into shape and being the means by which the various cropping programmes were tested over the years – as well as dealing with the frustrations that were an inevitable part of the process. Perhaps the most significant of these people, at different periods, have been Tom Petherick, Gillian Cartwright, Paul Haywood (bottom right) and Johanna Lausen-Higgins (top right), who have all moved on to pastures new and to areas of ever-greater endeavour. Their present successes and career moves are undoubtedly rooted in hard-won experience from those early days at Heligan. Now that our present team has settled into place, the tasks have become understood and the skills involved have become second nature, it is interesting to see that we have much the same number of staff as was here 100 years ago, and that these people are even organized in much the same way. We have not yet recovered the various glasshouse heating systems, so we can operate without the 24-hour staffing that used to be necessary for stoking and airing, but we still need to provide seven-day-a-week cover to maintain the garden. To the untrained eye, the gardens may look like Utopia, but there are always cracks requiring time and energy to repair, as the climate, the vagaries of seed germination, the predations of pests and diseases and the attentions of our furry and feathered friends wreak their havoc. The characteristic that binds the team members together, allowing individuals to work so effectively in harmony, is their interest in and affection for the place in which they work. They all, in their own ways, want the whole process to succeed – to create a harmonious whole and demonstrate their own commitments to the cause, thus providing an experience for the garden visitor which is second to none.

THE PLAYERS

Tim Smit is, quite simply, the man without whom this project would never have happened. It was he, as the founding father, who saw the possibilities, sought the relevant advice, recruited and put together the early personalities, secured the funding and always remained the driving force. The Lost Gardens of Heligan was his vision, however idealistic and blurred it might have been at that time!

In its early incarnation it inevitably stuttered, but succeeded because of Tim's ability to encourage and enthuse and never to take 'No' for an answer when the going got tough. When we started out on this journey, Tim had little or no understanding or knowledge of gardening; but he is a quick learner and even attempts to derail him by using Latin plant names failed to deter him. Now the driving force at the Eden Project, he is, of course, no longer involved with Heligan on a day-to-day basis, but his benign influence continues to permeate the whole philosophy. I am proud of his successes and to have been a member of both the Heligan and the Eden teams.

Heligan only operates effectively because it is a successful and profitable business. Such a situation is a rarity in the 'Gardens Open' business, where sensible, hard-headed, pragmatic decision-making is often lacking, abandoned in favour of sentiment, emotionally motivated actions and otherwise unviable options or preferences, often egotistically motivated. Heligan has been able to develop to its current happy state because of the leadership, direction and sensitive decision-making of the Managing Director, Peter Stafford. Although he is not a gardener, he understands all those components that are required to make a garden open to the public into a successful business and a 'fit for purpose' visitor attraction. He combines these qualities with a natural sympathy for all of the particular specialisms and capabilities of staff in all departments. Unusually for a manager, he recognizes especially those various empathies which are characteristic of the annual cycle of the gardening calendar, and the requirements for the continuing evolution and development of a project in which gardening is the core business. He is an excellent manager with natural, in-built business skills; but more importantly he is also a leader. Seldom are the two characteristics found in one person. The environment he has created allows an atmosphere in which all the staff, especially the gardeners, can operate on a stable and progressive basis, knowing the certainties which are derived from working within a sound business. The structure of the garden staff has evolved naturally over the years. Today, with as stable a financial base as is reasonably feasible, there are not the constraints which so often bedevil many such ventures, and a full complement of gardeners and tradesmen is allowable. This encourages and assures progress and stability, within reasonable limits.

The day-to-day management of the gardening team in the productive gardens is now vested in two fairly recently recruited young horticulturists, Sylvia Travers and Jeremy Pedersen (top right). Jeremy is the chief of the Vegetable Garden, and it is his job to implement the annual cropping plans each season. He has to manage his staff to carry out the cultivation, raise the crops, keep the area neat and tidy, beat the pests and diseases, and arrange the harvesting, among the myriad other tasks involved in a successful kitchen garden operation. He is on a steep learning curve! At the time of writing (late 2004) he has barely been in post for a year. Not only was he unfamiliar with Victorian kitchen gardening, he had never dealt with imperial measurements. However, he has a dedicated approach and is learning far more quickly than could be anticipated. He was born in Denmark and trained for four years in the Botanic Gardens in Copenhagen. He first worked with us as a student and has now returned as a permanent member of staff. His forte is in the seeking of advice – he so wants everything to be right first time.

Sylvia is Irish and first came to us on a student placement as part of her training at the Botanic Garden in Dublin. She also has a Master's degree in Anthropology. Sylvia has a very calm, collected and intellectual approach to

her job, coloured with considerable tact and diplomacy. She is responsible for the fruit, the glasshouses, cultivating the cucurbits and overseeing the Walled Garden – a job that includes some of the very specialized activities that are such a necessary part of our overall operations. She is also on a steep learning curve, but is dedicated to her work and recognizes the importance of achieving a practically founded skills base. It is comforting to have someone of her calibre among us.

The anchor for the Vegetable Garden, since very early on, has been Katharine Cartwright (above). In the early years especially, Kathy committed huge amounts of time and energy to ensuring that our cropping programmes were properly

Back from left: Haydn, Clive, Charles, Sylvia; front: Helen, Kathy, Philip, Mike and Annie, Summer 2004

implemented and that the minutiae were not forgotten, and she continually reminds us that a high-quality product is the main objective. It is she who emphasizes our commitment to a tradition and acts as the rock on which this is implemented, a repository of knowledge and experience to keep us all on the straight and narrow. She is truly committed to Heligan and is the 'Keeper of the Keys' in ensuring that the continued timelessness and the need for seamlessness in our annual activity are not forgotten. She, of all of us, is probably closest to our ideals.

Over the last couple of years, we have been able to recruit some very able, if as yet inexperienced, horticulturists, in order to create the beginnings of an efficient, knowledgeable and organized productive gardens team. This allows us to look to the future with confidence as they assume responsibility for their work and are able to take us onward while maintaining the tradition. Annie Carr came into the productive gardens team from the teams that operate in the southern gardens and the estate. She has quickly become an integral member, working chiefly in the Vegetable Garden where she is taking great pains to learn and increase her knowledge and skills. What she lacks in stature she makes up with dedication, hard work and a pursuit of the required knowledge.

In the Walled Garden we currently rely on the experience of two part-time workers, Helen Wilson and Caroline Green. Helen has considerable experience in organic vegetable and flower gardening, and brings a purposeful approach to all the tasks she undertakes. She has to juggle being a full-time mother with her work, but manages both responsibilities with stoic aplomb. She is fully committed to achieving the tasks required – woe betide anyone who appropriates her trowel! Caroline is a senior nurse who has decided to make a career-change into horticulture, but for whom the economic necessities of life mean that she has to juggle the two jobs to maintain a reasonable equilibrium. She started to gain the requisite background by joining the Eden Project on its first student intake and is now gaining practical experience to which she brings calmness and maturity.

During the peak season in the Summer we also offer students work placements in order to alleviate the pressures on the regular staff. Over the years we are fortunate to have recruited some very capable and committed people who carry out what may be seen as the more mundane tasks – humping manure and dragging seaweed, digging, grading, raking, hoeing, ridging, weeding, putting up the beanpoles, pea sticks, posts and wiring wherever needed, harvesting, and generally fetching and carrying. These jobs are, nevertheless, an essential part of preparing and maintaining the stage on which the plants perform. We depend on these people, with their very practical skills, to achieve so much of the basis on which our successful cropping depends.

Mike Rundle (right, with Philip) has been with us since the very early days when, like everyone involved, he lent his hand to whatever was required. He grew up in a farming background locally and in the course of a long career has been, among other things, a crane driver. Now approaching Senior Citizen status, he is the tractor-driver for the productive gardens: his tasks include collecting seaweed from Porthmellon, touring local stables for manure, and the general transport of anything that would have required horses in the past. He specializes in a number of tasks, the growing of potatoes – planting, ridging, harvesting, seed selection and storage – being his forte. He also thins root crops, erects the climbing bean canes, and hoes super-efficiently – an indispensable man who will turn his hand to whatever is needed, with a countryman's understanding. He is a forthright character who always bats his best for Heligan and kowtows to no man: it would be difficult to imagine the gardens without him.

Charles Fleming is another of the very early recruits who was responsible for planting the archway and wall fruit with me in the winters of 1993 and 1994.

Charles (below, in snow) was a printer from the days of hot lead. As technology progressed, the need for his skills disappeared, so he gravitated through various grant-aided systems to Heligan, where he has found his niche. He is a one-man crusade in our war against weeds, usually to be found on his knees in corners, along the sides of paths, under hedges, or along walls – anywhere they are trying to avoid detection. Charles also digs, is an indispensable member of the sea-weed-dragging team, and carries out numerous other tasks, usually managing to be in the right place when a film crew is around! He keeps a diary of his work at Heligan, which he publishes at his own expense. Like Mike he is part of the scenery.

Clive Mildenhall has progressed to the gardening team from his early days working in the car-park. This star darts player has become an indispensable member of the support brigade: he is now a skilled double-digger, potato man, post-and-wire specialist and pea-sticker. He is also the specialist label painter. The vast number of large, white, painted labels that we use require continual re-

furbishment and he sees to that by using periods of bad weather to advantage. He makes and repairs chitting trays and the like, and his *pièce de résistance* is stringing the garlic, shallots and onions for the annual Harvest Festival. He often presents a dour front, but every so often this is lightened by an almost angelic smile. These three men are very much of independent mind and are laws unto themselves; but without their dedication and commitment to the cause we could not succeed.

In the way of things at Heligan, people come for one job and end up moving to another. Such a person is Haydn Smith, who came to Heligan as part of the catering team and then 'discovered' gardening. He is a cheerful, wiry Welshman, who

seems to have determined his vocation relatively late in life. He undertakes whatever tasks are put his way with an innate understanding, and is always enquiring and learning. He was seconded to the garden one Autumn from the tearooms, has managed to avoid repatriation, and stays even in the foulest of weathers! One of our most important seasonal workers in the Winter is Emiliano Sanchez (bottom left), an Argentinian who spends his Summers as a star speedway rider and comes to us in the Autumn (when he is not in a number of pieces) to undertake vast areas of double- and single-digging. He is a cheerful man who turns his hand to whatever is required with willingness and good humour. His excavation of the soil in the beds in the Paxton House when the vines succumbed to disease and had to be replaced will go down in the Heligan gardening legend. This type of work suits his out-of-season training programme and helps to provide him with a diet of more than crusts.

It would be invidious of me to complete this description of the cast without mentioning our brave, skilled and indefatigable maintenance team led by Adrian Burrows. A group containing carpenters and joiners, stonemasons and bricklayers, painters and handymen, no task is too big or too small for them, and all undertake their work with skill and good humour. They carry out a whole spectrum of activities from much heavy civil engineering-type work (the replacement of sewers and drainage systems, for example) right through to the detailed tasks required in rebuilding glasshouses (as they did with the Melon House in the Autumn of 2003). Along the way they also find time to deal with the many small repair and maintenance tasks and day-to-day crises that beset any operation, and are inevitable in such an enterprise as Heligan. As a group they achieve monumental amounts of work – the replacement of the boardwalk in the Jungle during the late Winter of 2004 being a recent example. Adrian deals with all the requests that are thrown at him with extraordinary diplomacy: he has an innate understanding of the 'urgency' of each task and is expert at juggling an incredible number of balls in the air at the same time. His team includes Dave Bulbeck, Sandor Czako, Bob Mitchell, Lee Watkins, Keith Johns and Chris Inman, all of whom are highly skilled in their particular trades and carry out their tasks with quiet authority. Included in this group should be Nigel Hicks, our contract digger operator, who, by his skills and sure touch, saves the team endless hours of back-breaking and tedious navvy work.

Finally, I cannot go further without saying a few words about Candy Smit. Candy has always been part of the Heligan scene but has recently become more intimately concerned with the organization and management of the operation, taking up the position of Creative Director. She ensures that the general ethos of all our activities is preserved and that the Lost Gardens of Heligan always reflect the vision of the pioneers, while still allowing the philosophy to evolve in sympathetic ways. This position chiefly involves monitoring and determining what we call the 'visitor experience' and then providing feedback, in the hope that we will all take note. Candy achieves her ends by maintaining a quiet dignity and purpose, so carrying everyone with her. Like Kathy, she is another Keeper of the Keys who ensures that we do not lose sight of our *raison d'être*.

CHAPTER 3

SOFT FRUITS

The overall pattern of cropping within the kitchen garden is determined by the rotational master plan. The vegetables follow a conventional annual rotation, but the soft fruits, rhubarb, asparagus, seakale, cardoons and globe artichokes have to fit into their own, less frequent, programme of rotation. The soft fruits occupy a site for about 12 years and the others for a term of three or six years, alternating with each other, and then the whole swapping with the soft fruit. This area can also be integrated, rotationally, with the vegetable programme over the long term. Consequently, the size of the segments for all these crops has to be interchangeable.

During the Winter of 2001–02, the Vegetable Garden was at last pushed back to its original boundaries. This has provided the opportunity to reorganize the pattern and placement of the different crops to take account of the anticipated permanent arrangement for the various rotational patterns for the foreseeable future, as from the 2002 season.

BUSH FRUITS

The bush fruits are initially occupying the site along the western side of the garden, between the path and the hedge, where they are now housed in a skeleton support structure which can be netted during the fruiting season to provide a protective cage. Although this site tapers slightly from North to South, it still lends itself to this management. It has been incorporated into the cropping sequences since the 2002 season, and has been deeply cultivated and manured. The bushes – four of each variety – are planted on the square at five feet between the plants: this gives sufficient space for picking and cultivating. The bed is mulched with straw each year to conserve water and reduce weed growth. The gooseberries and currants (right) are grown mainly as bushes, but a small section of cordon-trained plants will be maintained to provide some very high-quality fruits.

During the nineteenth century, the culinary taste in bush fruits was for gooseberries and the red and white currants. Black currants were used chiefly to make cordials and to flavour medicinal concoctions, and did not become a major culinary crop until the very end of the century.

GOOSEBERRIES

The Victorian era saw the heyday of the development of the gooseberry, and it is still relatively easy to obtain stock of many of the old varieties: they have stood the test of time and have, of course, been the subject of specialist competition, especially in various areas of the Midlands and the North. The most obvious variation in gooseberry fruits is in their colour at maturity, hence the classification as red, green, yellow, or white. All gooseberries are green when immature, but ripen to the particular colour indicated if left on the bush. We have chosen three varieties of each colour to grow as bushes. All our stock is supplied by Rogers of Pickering, who are the foremost nursery producers of this material and still maintain a comprehensive collection of varieties.

In order to indicate the season of maturity for the crop, the following can be used as a guide: *Early*, from the end of June to mid-July; *Mid-season*, from mid- to late July; and *Late*, from the end of July into early August. However, considerable variation may occur, depending on the region of the country and the conditions of the local site.

Ironmonger, which dates from before 1825, has a spreading to drooping habit and produces prolific crops of relatively small, more or less oval, hairy fruits. It is mid-season in maturity and the fruit is of dessert quality. The gooseberries have an excellent, intense, rich flavour and a dull red colour.

Lancashire Lad has been described as 'probably the best all-round red gooseberry for garden or market purposes'. Developed c. 1824, it produces heavy crops of large, oblong-shaped, dark claret, hairy fruits. It is mid-season in maturity, and the fruit is of fair flavour for dessert quality but is normally picked green for cooking.

London (1831, top right) has a predominantly spreading habit with good yields of very large, long, oval, smooth-skinned, purple-red fruits of good flavour and dessert quality. It is a late-season variety and was widely used for exhibition and competition.

Howard's Lancer (1831) makes a large, spreading bush, which requires rigorous pruning to keep it controlled and in shape. It is an all-round variety in terms of use, producing enormous crops of large, oval, softly hairy, thin-skinned, transparent, greenish-white fruits at maturity. These have excellent flavour. It is a reliable cropper annually and the fruit matures in mid-season.

Keepsake (1841) is regarded as one of the most reliable varieties for early use, when it is picked green for cooking, as it bulks up quickly. It is a heavy cropper, producing large, oval, hairy, thin-skinned, pale green fruits of excellent flavour in the second-early season, when it is used for dessert purposes.

Langley Gage (*c.* 1897) has a distinctive habit of vigorous, strong, upright growth. It produces good crops of small to medium-sized, roundish, smooth,

pale silvery-green, transparent fruits of dessert quality in mid-season. These have a very sweet flavour.

Broom Girl, developed before 1852, is one of the best early-season gooseberries for dessert use. It produces very large, oval to roundish, hairy, dark yellow fruit with a good flavour. It is a regular cropper and develops a strong-limbed bush.

Early Sulphur (1825) produces early crops of medium-sized, oval to round, hairy, bright yellow, almost transparent, thin-skinned fruits, with an excellent flavour for culinary or dessert use.

Yellow Champagne (pre-1800) has an erect habit. It is a late-cropping variety which develops high yields of small, round, hairy, thin-skinned, yellow fruits of dessert quality with an excellent, rich flavour.

Careless (above right), dating from before 1860, was one of the most widely grown varieties in the UK during the twentieth century, much favoured for market growing. It develops into a vigorous, almost drooping bush that requires a judicious pruning regime to keep the centre open, as it is well armed. It produces heavy, mid-season yields of very large, oval, smooth-skinned, transparent, creamy or whitish-green fruits of good flavour, used mainly for culinary purposes.

(Cleworth's) **White Lion** makes a large, strong bush. It crops in mid-season and produces very large, oval but slightly flattened, downy, thin-skinned, white fruits with an excellent flavour for dessert or culinary use. In the twentieth century, between the wars, it was a significant market growers' variety.

(Woodward's) **Whitesmith** (pre-1824, above) is a mid-season variety of vigorous, upright habit, which produces heavy crops of fairly large, oval, virtually smooth, thin-skinned, whitish-green fruits with excellent flavour. It is one of the best all-round garden varieties, suitable for culinary or dessert use.

In the Victorian era, gooseberry bushes were grown on a single leg of nine inches or so before branching was allowed, raising the crown of the bush above the ground. This leg was, and still is, a necessary part of successful production, and is associated with the need to keep the surface of the soil free of all vegetation. Such attention to detail permits good air circulation around and through the bush and this, in turn, significantly reduces the incidence of the debilitating mildew diseases of the leaves – European gooseberry mildew and American gooseberry mildew. Infection is otherwise encouraged and will become rife if the still, humid conditions engendered are allowed to continue unchecked. Gooseberries are usually spiny and hostile bushes, but keeping them clean of weeds is essential. Picking can be an uncomfortable business, so the pruning technique is to create an open-centred bush with a goblet-shaped arrangement of branches. From this structure, the fruit hang down and can be picked from the outside with the minimum of personal discomfort. Gooseberries develop their flowers and fruit on old wood, which produces fruiting spurs; thus a semi-permanent structure needs to be created which will also provide the air circulation needed. Growing on a cordon system also reduces both the disease problem and the discomfort factor.

The principal pest of the gooseberry is the gooseberry sawfly. This becomes apparent when the caterpillars begin to eat the leaves fairly early in the season, and the effect can be quite devastating – the larvae defoliate a bush rapidly. Although insecticidal sprays can be used, continued observation and picking the small larvae from the bushes is very effective. Shaking the bushes so that the larvae fall off is also effective, as birds find and take them on the ground: to this end we pen the ducks in the gooseberry cage for the sawfly season! The adult insects can also (supposedly) be discouraged by using garlic sprays. Birds can damage some fruit, but their predations are by no means as severe as that experienced in the currant crop.

If really high-quality, large berries are required, it is usual to grow the plants as **single-stem cordons**. The object is to produce a single vertical stem with a series of short, lateral fruiting spurs. These spurs, and the number of berries on them, can easily be thinned to increase the size and quality of fruit produced. Cordon development can be achieved quite readily by planting rooted cuttings and training the leader shoot vertically up a cane, while competing shoots at the base are pruned away and the laterals on the cordon stem are shortened. Although this sounds a complex activity, it is actually quite straightforward and repays the extra effort. The height to which the cordon is taken is normally governed by practicality: up to eight feet is, perhaps, normal, but ten or 12 feet is possible if the plant is trained on a wall. The plants are usually sited about 18 ins. apart in the row, the canes being retained and supported by posts and a wire. Our rows are five feet apart and are oriented north-south. Such a pattern lines them up to correspond with the rows of bushes. It is prudent to select varieties which have a vigorous and upright habit for cordon growing, so that the need to tie in and provide support is minimized, but our selections have been chosen more for flavour and quality than for ease of training.

Leveller, introduced in 1851, is one of the best dessert varieties. It produces heavy crops of very large, oval to oblong, smooth, greenish-yellow fruits of excellent flavour. It crops during the mid-season and was used extensively for market growing during the inter-war years of the twentieth century, becoming the predominant dessert variety. It was also grown commercially as a cordon crop to produce premium quality fruit, in the East Grinstead area of Sussex. It is not particularly stiffly upright in habit, but its vigorous growth does respond well to cordon training. This variety also responds well to good soil conditions, and benefits from potash and organic nitrogen feeds.

Whinham's Industry (pre-1851, left) is a mid-season variety which produces medium to large, oval, hairy, dark red fruit with a fine and sweet flavour, good for both culinary and dessert use. As a cordon it produces high-quality dessert fruit and crops heavily. It has a stiff and upright habit that makes cordon training relatively easy.

RED AND WHITE CURRANTS

Red and white currants were highly prized and constituted two of the most desirable of the summer soft fruits of the Victorian era. They were grown extensively in the kitchen garden, both as bushes and as cordons. The diversity of selection was never in the same league as that of the gooseberry, largely because they were not the subject of competition and exhibition, so there are far fewer varieties to choose from; but a good spectrum of old varieties can still be found. The spacing of the plants, as either bushes or cordons, is the same as for gooseberries, and the system of pruning is effectively the same, as the plants flower on old wood and develop lateral, fruiting spurs. An open-centred, goblet-shaped bush provides good light characteristics, and hence high-quality fruits.

The major pest problems for currants are birds and aphids. Birds can quickly strip a bush of ripe fruit, and the only foolproof method of preventing this is to grow the crop in a cage (which needs to be covered only at fruiting time), or to have some system of netting individual bushes. This, however, has to be compatible with the need to be able to pick the crop easily. Birds become less of a problem in large-scale plantations as the population can only eat the same amount of fruit – a smaller proportion of the larger crop! Aphids cause the characteristic red, swollen, blister-like patches that appear on the leaves in the Summer. This infestation is not always on a serious scale but is nevertheless unsightly. Aphids can be controlled by spraying with a modern (targetted) aphidicide early in the season, as a routine precaution, or soft soap sprays can be used on a regular basis.

Picking currants requires some skill, and the crop is least damaged and most readily picked on the sprig. If an attempt is made to pick the mature crop as individual berries, many will burst with the minimum amount of pressure from fingers. The berries are most satisfactorily removed individually in the kitchen. The following varieties have been recruited for the new soft-fruit beds at Heligan:

Laxton's No. 1 develops into a strong, vigorous, upright bush with prolific spur production and consistently heavy yields. It fruits as a second-early/mid-season crop, producing a reliable yield of long bunches of very large, sweet, shining, scarlet fruits annually. It is being grown in our scheme both as a bush and as a cordon.

Red Lake (below) develops as an upright, moderately vigorous bush, with excellent spur production. It develops heavy yields, cropping reliably on an annual basis during the mid-season. It produces long trusses of large, round,

sweet, juicy fruits. It too is being grown as a bush and as a cordon.

White Versailles, introduced in 1843, has been one of the standard varieties of currant by which others have been measured for a long time. It develops as a moderately vigorous, upright bush with prolific spur production. Flowering very early, it sets fruit quickly and can develop immense crops on bunches up to four or five inches long. The fruits are large, round, very sweet and, at maturity, pale yellow in colour. It is used for both culinary and dessert purposes.

White Grape develops into a broad, upright bush with good spur production and heavy yields, and is being used as a cordon in our scheme. It produces large, round, very thin-skinned, very sweet, juicy, golden-tinted, white fruits. These are picked by removing the sprig, as the currants tend to burst if an attempt is made to pick them individually.

Our previous soft-fruit plantation also contained the following white currants, which were grown successfully. These varieties may well be replanted where space becomes available, and will probably end up as cordons, filling gaps on walls:

White Pearl (= **White Transparent**, above) produces large, yellowish, round fruits with a transparent skin through which the seeds are visible. The bunches are 3 ft. 6 ins. long.

White Dutch develops into a somewhat spreading bush and is of extremely old vintage. The bunches are about three inches long and produce fairly large, distinctly flattened, round, creamy white fruits. The fruits are juicy and sweet but somewhat tart.

BLACK CURRANTS

The black currant crop, although certainly grown during the latter half of the nineteenth century, was not nearly as important as the gooseberries and other currants, and in no way matched the popularity it achieved during the twentieth century. In a Victorian household, the principal use for this crop would have been to provide the basis of a cordial and to flavour medicines.

Black currants are invariably grown in bush form, and the pruning system is subtly different from that of red and white currants insofar as the most prolific fruit production occurs on second- and third-year wood. Although older wood will produce fruit, yield falls off dramatically. Pruning therefore requires the removal of three-year-old shoots, sufficient one-year-old stems being left as replacements. The cycle of shoot production is reliant on new stems being developed from the stem buds at the base of the bush, so the cuts should be made as low

down as possible when removing stems to keep the shape of the bush tidy and controlled. In general, the bushes tend to be fairly vigorous and are planted in rows eight feet apart with six feet between bushes in the row. The usual problem associated with growing black currants is that they flower early and the potential for cropping can be severely reduced by spring frost, but this is very rarely a problem in Cornwall.

At present, we grow two old varieties of black currant:

Baldwin (right) produces one of the smallest and most compact bushes for varieties of this vintage. It develops two or three racemes of flower from each spur, each with several (+/- eight) flowers. The berries are thick-skinned, of medium size, deep colour and good flavour. It has the advantage of flowering fairly late, so avoids frost, and crops in mid-season.

Boskoop Giant, raised in Holland in 1885 and introduced to the UK in 1895, develops as a tall, slightly spreading bush with relatively sparse foliage. It tends to produce only one raceme of fruit per spur, but this is long and carries many (15+) flowers. The berries tend to be large and, due to their very thin skins, have a propensity to burst easily. This is a poor quality for commercial use, but for the home gardener the absence of tough skins in cooking is a definite advantage. The berry colour is greenish-black (because of the thin skin), and the bushes crop during the early part of the season.

CANE FRUITS

The cultivation of cane fruits in the kitchen garden was not high on the agenda until towards the end of the nineteenth century.

RASPBERRIES

The raspberry is a native of woodland conditions and, as such, tolerates semi-shade in the garden while still cropping well. The cultivation and management of the raspberry crop is based on the particular growth cycle of the plant. This depends on the fact that a sucker cane develops from a stem bud produced on a root during the early Spring. The sucker grows vigorously during the first season and sets its fruit buds at the end of that Summer, before entering a dormant period during the Winter. In the early Summer of the second year the cane flowers and fruits. This cane is then pruned out to allow the present season's new canes to mature; and so the cycle continues.

The raspberry requires plenty of moisture to produce a prolific crop: it is needed to enhance the swelling of the fruit, which occurs quite rapidly. The crop therefore benefits from mulching, which greatly improves moisture conservation in the soil. The curtain method of training the canes, more or less universal today, is a relatively recent development: in the nineteenth century they were grown in clumps around a central stake. The young canes were tied to the stake while the fruiting ones were free to lean outwards, presenting the fruit for picking.

Norfolk Giant is one of the few named varieties surviving from the late nineteenth century and is still available (just). It has tall canes, which are vigorous when free from viruses, and produces its new annual canes from close in the stool rather than as root suckers. The fruits are small to medium-sized, narrow conical, dull deep red, firm, juicy and with a tart flavour. It crops during the late season and produces heavy yields.

Yellow Antwerp is a very old variety with quite large, roundish, bright yellow fruits which have a good flavour.

Cornish White is a virus-riddled stock, but is grown to perpetuate a white (actually pale creamy yellow) raspberry found in many Cornish gardens. One day we will get round to having it 'cleaned up'. The stems are covered in dense bristles – is this **White Magnum Bonum** of the old books?

BLACKBERRY

Although many blackberries were undoubtedly picked from the hedgerows, it was necessary to grow a few high-quality berries in the kitchen garden. In the past we have grown blackberries on posts and wires, but they took more space than was warranted and are now being trained on wires on the back of the Melon Yard wall at the bottom of the Vegetable Garden. Their culture is relatively simple: the

fruiting stems are removed and replaced annually by vegetative stems of the current season.

Himalayan Giant is an old selection and is very vigorous and thorny. It produces heavy crops of large, black, shiny berries from mid-August onwards, for about three weeks. It is admirably suited to jam-making and bottling, but is used chiefly as a dessert fruit.

LOGANBERRY

The loganberry (previous page) was a very late nineteenth-century introduction from North America. It is a hybrid berry whose habit of growth and cultivation are the same as those of the blackberry. The fruits are large, cylindrical and raspberry-coloured, and are picked with the plug intact. The season lasts longer into September than that of blackberries. There is also a thornless clone.

STRAWBERRIES

Traditionally, the main strawberry crop was expected in mid-summer, but was spread over a longer period of time by simple advancing and retarding techniques. It was also cropped under glass for Christmas by rooting and establishing runners in mid-summer.

Until the second half of the nineteenth century, strawberry plants were routinely raised from seed, but by the end of the century scores of varieties had been selected and were raised from runners. Of these extensive selections few varieties have survived and only one, **Royal Sovereign** (top right, in flower) is available commercially. **Sir Joseph Paxton** (1862) is probably the only other variety of relevant vintage still extant, although not available.

The strawberry is propagated from runners which develop naturally after fruiting. Under normal circumstances these are removed by cutting back to the crown at an early stage of development, in order to channel all the food reserves into the crown. This enhances flower-bud initiation and so forms the basis of a good crop the following year. The operation is a continuous and tedious task over the second half of the Summer, but greatly enhances the fruiting potential.

Our main crop is grown in the open ground of the Vegetable Garden, in a series of five beds, each six feet wide. The prime requirement of these beds is to manage annually an efficient and sufficient strawberry production. The crop is usually cultivated on a three-row bed system, with the rows 18 ins. apart and the plants in the row at 18-ins. intervals. However, the combination of our highly fertile soil and fresh, virus-free plants has caused us to re-evaluate this spacing, as the vigour of the plants has been phenomenal. We now grow the strawberries on a two-row bed, with the rows three feet apart and the plants 15 ins. apart: any closer and the dense growth invariably paves the way for damp conditions among the leaves which encourages grey mould rot (*Botrytis*) on the fruits.

The crop is grown on a rotational basis within the five beds. In order to maintain it in a healthy, virus-free condition, it is sensible to buy in fresh stock (i.e. rooted runners) annually from a registered grower producing certified virus-free material. The rotation starts with a well-manured crop of early potatoes to clean the land. This is followed, in mid-summer, by the planting of the pot-grown runners. The runners are purchased in early Spring, when they are potted up and maintained for the few weeks until planting out. After planting, and when the crowns are established, the plants are de-blossomed and de-runnered for the remainder of the season. Each year in early September the plants are sheared over and all the vegetation is removed. This also allows the crowns to have the runner stubs cleaned away and, if necessary, the crowns can be thinned. The plants are cropped for the following two seasons, and are removed as soon as fruiting has finished at the end of the second of these seasons (i.e. in year three). A catch crop is then taken in the second half of the Summer. In year four, a crop of gladioli and ixias is taken, and in year five the bed is used as a winter leek seedbed and for a maincrop of spring onions before returning to year one and the early potatoes. Under this regime there are two fully productive beds of fruiting plants in each year. It is necessary to create such a rotational programme in order to minimize the potential for the spread of root-borne diseases, which can be a problem with strawberries.

Sylvia picks strawberries in the Vegetable Garden

The cropping season may be advanced by growing and forcing the crop in a cold frame, as we also do in the Melon Yard (below). The crop is planted as pot-grown runners just after mid-summer, and allowed to establish. Plant growth can be accelerated by covering the frame in the early Spring when the weather is warm and sunny. The frame should be aired by venting the lights at the top end, in order to lower the humidity and so reduce the incidence of grey mould on the fruit. This disease is a scourge and warm, humid conditions only encourage it to spread rapidly. After fruiting, remove the lights and allow the foliage to flourish by proper attention; then shear off all the vegetation in late August, clear away any runners, thin the crowns if necessary, and allow the new foliage to develop. A late-season crop would have been achieved by growing the crop in a cooler situation (under a north wall) and/or by using a late-cropping variety. No suitable period-correct varieties are available, so we have used **Cambridge Late Pine** in the past.

Royal Sovereign (1892), for years the standard for flavour, still has not been overtaken as the benchmark against which all other varieties are compared by the cognoscenti. It is white-fleshed, with a bright, almost scarlet, red fruit colour.

The yields, by today's standards, are rarely more than good, but the fruit has the traditional flavour of a sweet but slightly tart strawberry, even when fully ripe. This variety (together with **Cambridge Favourite**) was the predominant commercial variety in the UK until the 1960s or early 1970s. It is particularly susceptible to viral disease and needs to be renewed from certified mother stock for each crop. It is not wise to propagate from home-grown runners more than once, and then only if the crop is showing no obvious symptoms of disease. It develops into a rather small, flat plant with light green leaves. The berries are soft and easily bruised, so by modern standards are not suitable for market purposes. These characteristics eventually led to Royal Sovereign's demise as a commercial variety. Today's varieties are bred to produce a high yield of fruit which can survive being packed and then transported long distances to market; hence the berries are firm and rubbery and, although their flesh is red, they have less flavour. Royal Sovereign is currently produced by a few nurserymen and is thus still available to the amateur gardener.

The **alpine** or **perpetual-fruiting strawberry** was also probably tucked away somewhere, but currently we do not grow it.

CHAPTER 4
STONE FRUITS

Most of the tree fruits that we grow are termed 'top fruits', and virtually all are members of the *Rosaceae*, the rose family. The stone fruits – almond, apricot, cherry, plum, peach and nectarine – are characterized by having a fleshy fruit enclosing a 'stone', which contains the seed. In general they require more warmth to mature their fruits to full flavour and quality than do the pome fruits (apples, pears, etc.) and hence are often given the advantage of a south-facing wall or a greenhouse.

When trained on a wall, stone fruits are traditionally grown in a fan-trained pattern, as this allows the pruning strategy of providing replacement fruiting wood to be most readily achieved. The building of a fan-trained specimen is not rocket science, but it does require a certain understanding of tree growth and where and when the flower buds are produced on these species of tree. It is best to start with a maiden whip – i.e. a one-year-old grafted tree with a single stem. Grafting on to a rootstock controls the vigour of the tree and may also provide resistance to pests and diseases or tolerance of particular soil conditions. The purchase of a so-called fan-trained tree does not always deliver a well-, or even correctly, prepared plant: indeed, the specimen may be no more than a normal branching tree that has been trained flat and resembles a herring bone. The home production of a fan is more time-consuming than difficult, and it takes patience and understanding over three or four years to produce a minimal structure. Nevertheless, the results are satisfying and produce a readily managed tree, and the processes soon become understood and ingrained. (For a guide to the production of a correctly developed tree see the RHS *The Fruit Garden Displayed*, or other reliable fruit manual.)

In general, the fan-trained fruit trees which we have attempted to grow since 1994 have proved to be a disaster in terms of their progress and proper development, mostly due to our inability to provide the required attention to detail in the early days and then, latterly, to provide a consistent management with a single person remaining in charge for more than a year or two. This has resulted in us 'biting the bullet' and grubbing up most of the trees (over a two- or three-year programme) to start again. New stock is being established with a single person, Sylvia, managing them, under the watchful and experienced eye of our consultant

guru, George Gilbert. We look forward to the future with an expectation of an enhanced experience of new flavours on a regular basis.

Many of the varieties of these subjects can be, and indeed are, grown as conventional, free-standing orchard trees in open situations. In such cases, the tree is grafted on to a 'free' or vigorous rootstock and is grown on to become a full-blown standard tree, the branching system not usually being allowed to start until a five- or six-foot trunk has been produced.

APRICOTS

The apricot is undoubtedly the most rewardingly delicious of the stone fruits grown outside, but the fruits need to be tree-ripened to achieve perfection. The benign, late-summer climate of Cornwall is ideal for apricots grown on a sunny, south-facing wall – indeed, there is no particular reason why they could not be grown as free-standing trees in a warm, sheltered position. They prefer limey, well-drained, but water-retentive soil conditions. Virtually any site proposed for apricot cultivation in Cornwall has acid soil, and it is therefore imperative to add lime and check the pH regularly. Apricots are self-fertile, but it is prudent to hand-pollinate in order to ensure a good crop, as there may be only a few insects around at their early flowering season.

During the early days at Heligan, we failed to give the apricots sufficient attention and they are thus being replanted and re-established from maiden trees. The varieties cited have been worked on **St Julien A** rootstocks in order to constrain vigour (as both varieties are vigorous growers) and so ease management.

Moorpark was introduced by Admiral Anson in 1760. Two fan-trained trees are being grown in the Walled Garden, on a wall with a southerly aspect. The fruits are large, and mature in early September. They are round, often slightly flattened, with a fairly deep suture; the skin is orange-yellow with a brownish-red flush on the sunny side, and the flesh is firm, juicy and orange-red in colour. During the nineteenth century this variety was prized as the best apricot in terms of flavour. It crops regularly and prolifically, as well as being large-flowered and very decorative.

New Large Early was raised by Thomas Rivers in 1873 and has a self-descriptive name. It crops from the end of July to early August. The large fruits are roundish to oval; the skin pale orange-yellow, with the hint of a red flush on the sunny side; the flesh bright orange, firm, 'melting' and juicy, with an excellent flavour. It crops regularly and is prolific.

CHERRIES

Cherries are notoriously unreliable to grow as a consistent crop because of a range of challenges. In general the conventional, 'up-country' cherries require deep, fertile soil in order to grow and crop well, and are therefore restricted to the brick-earth soils of northern Kent and like places, which also have low annual rainfall. Birds are a particular problem, not only because they love to strip the trees of ripe fruit in no time flat, but also because the buds are devastated in early Spring by birds such as bullfinches. Cherry trees are prone to several types of disease – fungal (silver leaf), bacterial (canker) and viral (shot hole and rubbery wood) – which can be widespread and can cause great damage. Conventional cherry trees were also large, making the fruit difficult to pick, but today this is not such a problem with the availability of reliable dwarfing rootstocks. To top all of this, cherries are not usually self-fertile and therefore require cross-pollination – and the interrelationships of this character are interesting!

SWEET CHERRIES

The warm, damp climate of Cornwall is not conducive to the successful growing of sweet cherries, but we persevere. We are attempting to grow two or three fan-trained cherries, but in order to give ourselves a sporting chance we are using the modern varieties **Stella** and **Merton Glory**, grafted on to **Colt**, a dwarfing rootstock. We are also growing **Early Rivers** of the old types. In the orchards we have **Governor Wood**, **Napoleon** and **Waterloo**, all growing on seedling *Prunus avium* rootstocks; but they struggle and we will probably dispense with them in due course.

SOUR (OR ACID) CHERRY

The **Morello** cherry is the commercial type of cherry used for flavouring cherry brandy. In the garden it is grown for use both in cooking and for flavouring. We are growing a fan-trained specimen on a north-facing wall at the bottom of the Vegetable Garden, where it grows vigorously and crops prolifically (if we net it against the birds). Its almost pure white blossoms, early in the Spring, herald the productiveness of the season to come.

TAMAR VALLEY CHERRIES

The Tamar Valley was long famous for the quantity of the cherry orchards which hugged its steep slopes. Because of these slopes, men were employed late in each Winter to shovel up the soil washed down and return it to the top using old-fashioned winches and steam engines. The varieties in the orchards were very local in distribution, and probably originated from early importations of trees from France in the days when cherries were little more than improvements on the wild *Prunus avium*. Those still extant today are selections from these, most made during the nineteenth century. It is difficult to know how many varieties existed originally, as the orchards were effectively unviable by the Second World War, and became abandoned and lost in rapid order. They were not conventional cherries but a race that the local farmers had developed to suit the thin soils and damp climate, while making use of the warm Spring. The Tamar Valley cherries fruited a week or ten days earlier than the varieties grown up country, giving the Cornish growers a market advantage. The trees were very upright, single-trunked specimens which could attain at least 40 ft., so that the fruit had to be picked from huge, heavy, 40-rung, wooden ladders: imagine the Health and Safety palaver this would raise today! The usual spacing for these trees is described as 'between 11 and 12 yards', but often this was not enough for mature specimens. The fruits themselves were small, black and sweet, and extraordinarily heavy-cropping. Such was the extent of production that boat trips were run up and down the Tamar for sightseers during the blossom season – this was still happening in the 1950s when I was a youngster – and, once rail transport had become commonplace, the cherries were harvested in sufficient quantities to be marketed all over the country.

The survival of these varieties, which rapidly came to the verge of extinction once their commercial use was abandoned by the late 1950s, can be attributed to James Armstrong-Evans and Mary Martin of St Dominic. They have scoured the area, visiting the relics of old orchards and talking to many old-time farmers, and done their utmost to save as many types as is feasible. They have attempted description and identification, typically based only on anecdotal evidence, and have re-propagated old varieties with a passion and single-mindedness which is a beacon for us all. We have four of these varieties in our orchard, and the descriptions which follow are theirs:

Birchenhayes is the earliest variety to mature, and crops up to two weeks before Burcombe. It has very attractive, shiny black fruits with green stems, of dessert quality and a sweet flavour.

Bullion ripens just after Burcombe. It has dark, reddish-black, large cherries with a very long stem. It is a very turgid fruit and splits easily. It is of dessert quality, with a slightly tangy, sweet flavour.

Burcombe was the standard, heavy-yielding, maincrop variety, cropping during the third or fourth week of July, and was popular for bottling as well as for dessert use. It is a black cherry with medium-sized fruits and a sweet flavour. It produces a stout tree with heavy limbs at a 45° angle.

Fice is also a maincrop variety, producing an elegant upright tree with very juicy black fruits of the highest dessert quality – unfortunately too juicy for marketing over any distance.

PLUMS AND GAGES

The name 'plum' covers a diverse group of stone fruits derived from wild plums and native species such as the sloe and the bullace. The group comprises plums, gages, damsons, bullaces and mirabelles (myrobalans). Most of our conventional plums and gages are descended from varieties imported from the Low Countries and Italy during the sixteenth century. In Cornwall, however, there are a number of peculiarly local selections which cope more readily with local conditions. The name gage, which is a generic description for the green and pale yellow, more or less transparent fruits, with their distinctive flavour, derives from Sir Thomas Gage, who imported the **Reine Claude** from France. This in itself is a very old variety dating from at least the Middle Ages, the French name commemorating the wife of Francis I. Other colours have since been introduced as a result of breeding, but are still distinguished by their flavour.

The following varieties are being grown as fan-trained trees on the front and back walls of the Melon Yard: they are currently very young and in the process of formation. The dessert gages are being grown on the south wall as they particularly benefit from the warm conditions, which enhance the flavours in the ripe fruit.

Denniston's Superb, introduced in 1835, is a medium- to large-sized, dessert greengage, of American origin, which matures in mid-August. The fruits are roundish-oval with a shallow, broad suture. The skin is greenish-yellow with dark green streaks, and the flesh yellowish-green, transparent and of excellent flavour. This self-fertile variety is a regular and reliable cropper, as well as being a good pollinator for others.

Early Transparent Gage was raised by Thomas Rivers and introduced in 1866. It is a dessert greengage type with small to medium-sized, round fruits, flattened at each end and having a very shallow suture, which mature in mid-August. The skin is pale apricot-yellow with crimson spots and a pale yellow bloom, and the flesh golden-yellow, transparent and with an excellent, rich greengage flavour. A heavy-cropping, self-fertile variety.

Czar, raised and named by Rivers in 1874, is a medium-sized, culinary plum, maturing in early August on a north wall. The fruits are roundish-oval, flattened at each end, with a deep suture, and have dull, bluish-red skins with limited bloom. The flesh is yellow-green and somewhat grainy. An excellent cropper, it is self-fertile and produces an abundance of fine, culinary quality fruit with deep red juice.

Rivers Early Prolific is a small to medium-sized culinary plum, raised by Thomas Rivers *c.* 1830. At Heligan it is grown on a north wall, and the round-oval fruit mature at the end of July. The plums have a shallow suture, deepening as it reaches the eye; the skin is dark purple-blue with a pronounced bloom, and the flesh is firm, juicy and golden-yellow. Although it is self-fertile, the variety benefits from pollinators. It rarely suffers from silver leaf disease but is an irregular cropper.

Victoria is a large, excellent quality, dual-purpose plum maturing in September. This variety was raised by Messrs Rivers and introduced *c.* 1860. The fruits are elongated oval with minimal suture, and the pale yellow skins have pinkish-brown flushes on the sunny side. Greenish-white in colour, flushed at the stone, the flesh is juicy, with a very rich, sweet flavour. A good cropper under sheltered conditions and self-fertile, this plum is, however, prone to silver leaf disease and bacterial canker. It is grown on the south wall, both to encourage ripening during the late season and to enhance flavour, and is one of the best quality all-round varieties.

The following varieties have been grown as field trees in an orchard situation, on a standard stem where habit permits. These trees can be found along the lane to the Old Kennels and survive from the 1996 plantings. Most of the remaining fruit trees have been resited.

Old Greengage is the original and well-recognized English greengage, with virtually transparent, pale green fruits in August and that unmistakable, aromatic flavour.

Orleans is a very old French variety, which used to be found all over the UK. It is not of the highest quality, but is a trouble-free and tenacious tree, regularly seen surviving in old Cornish orchards. It bears small to medium-sized, culinary-grade plums, which mature in mid-August. The fruit is round but marginally flattened at both ends; the skin deep blue-black with a heavy bloom and shallow suture, and the flesh pale yellow, both sweet and tart.

Warwickshire Drooper is one of the better quality 'up-country' selections, which, in Cornwall, has consistently proved to be the most successful cropper, being free of disease and forming a tenacious, prolific, hardy tree, able to survive considerable competition. It produces medium- to large-sized, dual-purpose plums that mature towards the end of August and into September. The fruits are oval and have a yellow skin dotted with red and a browny-pink flush on the sunny side. They have a reasonable gage-type flavour, and are used for cooking or bottling towards the end of August: by September they are a very acceptable dessert fruit.

Black Kea is a plum peculiarly local to an area south of Truro in the villages of Kea, Coombe and Cowlands. It is probably more of a bullace than a conventional plum. It was used to make Black Kea plum jam, a traditional local product, on a commercial basis until the 1950s. The fruits are produced prolifically during August and early September, on a tree that varies from a spiny, thicket-like tall shrub to a normal-sized tree. This variety is more a strain than a clone, as many trees have obviously arisen from self-sown seed – normally the superior forms are propagated from suckers. The fruits are more or less round with a blue-black skin and white bloom. The flesh is yellow with a tart flavour. It can also be used to make wine and a spirit.

Red Kea is another culinary plum of the same provenance as the black variety, although it is not a bullace, and when fully ripe it is acceptable for dessert purposes. Now fairly uncommon, it forms an upright large bush or small tree which would probably not be grown (although it is readily propagated from suckers) but for its unusual origins. The small, oval fruits have a shallow suture, dull red skin, and yellow flesh with a reasonable flavour.

Porthscatho Grey is a local variety from the southern tip of the Roseland Peninsula that has survived on account of its local connection. The fruits are medium in size, long oval in shape, and have brown skins with pale greenish lenticels. It is definitely a cooking plum!

Manaccan is a prolific, local plum from the Lizard Peninsula, specifically the area around the village of Manaccan. It is unusual in producing clusters of fruit, giving the impression of grapes. The plums are small, roundish, yellow fruits with a pink flush on the sunny side and minimal sutures. The yellow flesh has a good flavour. It is a relatively tall, upright tree, with a distinctive pale green mature bark. Its suckering habit makes it easy to propagate.

CHAPTER 5

POME FRUITS

In addition to the stone fruits, the other major top fruit crops are the pome fruits – also members of the *Rosaceae*. These have fleshy fruit, which often has a highly coloured skin when ripe and contains several small, dryish seeds in the core. This group includes the apples, pears, quinces, medlars and, at Heligan, an unusual, semi-wild gathered fruit, from the genus *Sorbus*, the otmast.

This group of top fruits is hardier and more easily grown, in general, than the stone fruits: the pome fruits mature and ripen more readily in our cool temperate climate. However, the very damp and warm climate of the far South-west creates ideal conditions for the development and spread of the major diseases of this group of trees – canker, scab and mildew – which is why apples and pears are grown commercially in the drier areas of the country. Despite this, apples have been, and still are, grown successfully in Cornwall. This success depends on the fact that a few of the conventional up-country varieties still to be found in Cornish orchards have a low susceptibility to disease, so grow and crop quite adequately here. The vagaries of the climate and the types of soil in the far South-west have also prompted growers to make many selections from the local, endemic varieties in Cornwall and South-west Devon which can cope with local conditions. These varieties have never been catalogued and described in any detail: knowledge of them is held largely by many of the old-timers, who are also disappearing. As old orchards become derelict and the trees are destroyed, this priceless resource is in danger of being lost. However, there is hope: a few enthusiasts are attempting to collect together the best old varieties, collate any relevant information, and propagate new stock for the future.

Pears have been less successful in adapting to the climatic problems of the area than apples and, because most of the conventional varieties, largely of French origin, are susceptible to disease, very few are seen. **Swan's Egg** is the significant exception.

APPLES

Apples are the most predominant of the pome fruits, and are grown in a variety of contexts. They are first seen in the gardens at Heligan as the trained trees which

create the archway down the axis of the Vegetable Garden, then as cordon-trained trees on part of the walls of the Melon Yard, and lastly and most extensively, in the orchards as standard trees.

APPLES ON THE ARCHES IN THE VEGETABLE GARDEN

The trees on the central archway of the Vegetable Garden were the second group of fruit trees to be planted, very early on in the restoration process. This particular situation required them to be on dwarfing rootstocks in order to control their vigour. The choice of varieties was thus limited to those which, at that time, could be chosen from commercially available sources and from those varieties which (a) had the least susceptibility to disease and (b) were grafted on suitable dwarfing rootstocks. The trees were trained over the arches to make a tunnel effect, and knee-high branches were trained laterally to make a line above the box hedge, which was planted beneath as an edging. This pattern of growing is traditional: the central path through the Vegetable Garden was developed to enhance the enjoyment of the proprietor and his guests while on a tour of the garden. Usually the trees trained in such situations were pears, but, being situated in Cornwall we felt that disease would be too much of a problem, so decided that apples would be a more prudent choice.

The pattern of planting is a block of four (two trees on either side) down the path at ten feet apart. The following varieties have been planted in the order given from the top to the bottom of the path: **Devonshire Quarrenden** (page 73), **Ribston Pippin** (top left), **Arthur Turner** (top right), **Rev W. Wilks**, **Charles Ross** (mid right), **Laxton's Epicure** (bottom left), **Laxton's Fortune** (bottom right), **Lord Derby** (mid left), **Ellison's Orange** and **American Mother**. Descriptions of these varieties (which are all period-correct) are available from readily accessible sources. What was a surprise, to me at least, was the overwhelming preference among the garden staff for the two Laxton varieties when they eventually fruited: these are the favourite eating apples for the lunch break!

The trees were planted, as maiden whips, during the Winter of 1994–95, the order of the varieties along the path being dictated

by the period of flowering. The earliest to flower are placed at the top, and the latest at the bottom of the path (top left), so that, should a late spring frost be experienced, the drainage of cold air and its build-up behind the wall at the bottom of the slope is less damaging to buds which have yet to break.

The initial development of these trees was undertaken by Paul Haywood. By the 2001 season, Johanna (bottom left) had built on this basis and perfected the management of these trees so that opposite pairs met at the apex of the arch, the laterals met to produce a continuous line (top left) and, as a result of proper pruning over the years, sufficient maturity

had developed to reward us with plentiful, highly coloured fruit on each arch, seven years after planting.

APPLES IN THE MELON YARD

The first group of trees to be planted were those to be trained as single cordons on the west-facing wall of the Melon Yard (on following pages, with heliotrope). Initially, the wall was dressed with brackets and horizontal wires, at one-foot intervals. Trees on dwarfing rootstocks were planted in the Winter of 1993–94 at intervals of three feet, leaning about 60° from the horizontal towards the South, and were held in place by tying into a cane angled across the wall. After two years, the angle of the trunk was decreased each year until it reached 45° from the horizontal. In the early years, extension growth is needed to reach a full length: such growth is achieved by the tree being as close to upright as is feasible. Once this is achieved, the angle away from the vertical is increased to enhance flower-bud production and reduce extension growth. The choice of these trees was determined by the commercial availability of suitable varieties grafted on to a relevant dwarfing rootstock. The following were planted and are now cropping: **Newton Wonder**, **Egremont Russet**, **American Mother**, **Norfolk Royal**, **Irish Peach**, **Ashmead's Kernel**, **Blenheim Orange**, **Orleans Reinette** and **Sturmer Pippin**.

ENDEMIC APPLE VARIETIES FROM THE FAR SOUTH-WEST

The opportunity to grow trees in a traditional format in an orchard situation – i.e. as standard trees at a relevant spacing – allowed us to indulge in the conservation of several indigenous Cornish varieties of apple.

It is generally assumed by the up-country pundits that any serious attempt to grow apples in Cornwall is, at best, imprudent and, at worst, a waste of time. This assumption is based on their perception of the climate and the selection of available varieties, but it demonstrates a degree of ignorance of the actual situation – most obviously that a considerable quantity of fruit trees is, and long has been, grown in Cornwall. There are many old and semi-derelict orchards still to be seen in the far South-west, and perusal of old tithe and Ordnance Survey maps gives an idea of the sizeable area covered by orchards in the past – until the Second World War, several thousand acres. Most farms and homesteads boasted an orchard of two or three acres, well protected by shelter hedges and used, because of this shelter, for lambing during the late Winter and Spring. The grass keep and shade also provided a place to house the rams during the Summer before the tupping season began. It was an important sanctuary for another staple of the domestic economy – the bees, with their contribution of honey and wax.

Of course it never was, and still is not, an easy proposition to succeed with orchard growing in Cornwall. It is well known that the mild and moist climate encourages the development of those scourges of the orchard, the fungal diseases canker, scab and mildew, as well as the proliferation of insect problems such as aphids and codling moth. It is also apparent that the soils are thin and acidic, and that the trees have to withstand strong winds loaded with salt and, sometimes, sand. Lesser mortals would have given up trying, but the need to win a varied food supply from the land led to a very local and specialized crop development.

During the 200 years before the Second World War, it had been the practice to sow apple seeds regularly in the garden. When these had germinated they were transplanted out into the farm hedgerows. After a few years of maturing, the fruiting potential of the new trees could be assessed, and the good forms lifted and moved into the orchard. Inevitably, superior selections were propagated and passed around, and they would also have received descriptive names in order to identify them. But, in general, these varieties tended to remain localized unless they were extraordinarily significant and were picked up by somebody of influence – Charles Hawkins' recognition of **Cornish Gilliflower** is a case in point. This development of a local spectrum of varieties has left Cornwall with a palette of excellent and well-adapted selections, and it is still not unusual to see apple trees in hedgerows in the remoter parts of the county.

This practice has given rise to several lines or series of seedlings, in which particular characteristics have become prevalent and very similar seedling trees occur; but two lines in particular can be singled out for attention. The first is found chiefly in the West and is a series descended from **Devonshire Quarrenden**. These apples are chiefly of the **Ben's Red** type, and typically produce small, more or less flattened, round, red fruits, of second-early maturity, on small, bushy trees. The second line is found around the Truro and St Austell area, and can be described as the **Polly** type. These are small, roundish to slightly conical, yellow, second-early season apples, on smallish, lightweight and upright trees. In both sets, a narrow spectrum of seedling characteristics is involved. It is just possible that, in most cases, both types are a highly volatile series of apomictic seedlings.

The range of local varieties is extremely diverse, and many are of high calibre by any standards. They include varieties suitable for culinary use, dessert, dual-

purpose, cider production and pickling, all of these maturing over a seasonal spectrum, and some with excellent keeping qualities. The spring-blossoming season tends to occur over a lengthy period, but in a Cornish orchard the sheer diversity of varieties, and the fact that they are virtually all diploid, tend not to create difficulties with pollination. Interestingly, many of these varieties also have a capacity for stem rooting (because they develop dormant, adventitious roots in the stems near the branch junctions) and so are easily propagated, without the need for grafting.

Traditionally, these apples would be grown as standard trees with a five- or six-foot-tall, clear trunk, and spaced at up to 30 ft. apart in a grassed orchard. They would be worked on 'free' (seedling) rootstocks to give maximum vigour: today we use **M25**. I believe that this freedom and the lack of stress, which would be developed on more dwarfing stock, contributes to a greater disease-tolerance. The trees should not be pruned (major surgery excepted), so that few wounds are produced and canker becomes less prevalent.

The origins of apples in this province are obscure, but it is highly probable that varieties were imported to the UK from Normandy and Brittany, accessible areas which had become important centres for the improvement of French production in the mid-eighteenth century, when interest in the improvement

Apple harvest display

of apples was developing. The clue to these origins is provided by the use of the word 'Quarrenden', or derivatives such as 'Quarentine', in varietal names. This is reputed to be a corruption of 'Carentan', an important Norman centre of apple-growing. In Cornwall and Devon this name was used regularly and without particular relevance, in the same way as Pippin (literally, 'seedling').

An overview of the varieties growing in a Cornish orchard shows that the palette is not totally made up of local varieties. It is evident that many of the up-country varieties, developed during the eighteenth and nineteenth centuries, were brought to Cornwall by local nurserymen and were tried out in local orchards. Many succumbed quickly to disease, but a few demonstrated resistances and tolerances and stayed to be part of the scene, notably **Astrakhan Red**, **Beauty of Bath**, **Blenheim Orange**, **Bramley Seedling**, **Gascoyne's Scarlet**, **Gladstone**, **Golden Noble**, **Lady Sudeley**, **Miller's Seedling** and **White Transparent**. The remnants of these can still be found in semi-derelict orchards.

A SELECTION OF LOCAL VARIETIES OF APPLE

The number of varieties of local apples is probably close to 150; but not even the most biased of Cornishmen will claim they are all of the highest calibre. There are no written descriptions of these varieties, so their identification is necessarily based on anecdotal evidence. Once they are identified it is possible, given time and inclination, to describe them. The beginnings of the recovery and reintroduction of these varieties must be attributed to James Armstrong-Evans and Mary Martin of St Dominick, who have been searching for and propagating them for more than 25 years, and without whose enthusiasm the rest of us would never have become engaged in growing the fruit. At Heligan, varieties of this type are nearly all planted within the Poultry Orchard (right), or have been transferred from our trial nut walk to the new Horsemoor Orchard, below the Old Kennels. Here is a selection:

CULINARY VARIETIES

Blackamoor Red is a large, marginally locular, flattened round fruit, not unlike a Bramley. The skin is of a green ground colour, eventually suffused with a deep red flush and veining. A culinary apple with a good, sharp flavour, it is a late-season variety which keeps through to Easter and is relatively disease-free. It develops as a vigorous, upright tree, tending to a single trunk. It is a reliable cropper.

Colloggett Pippin (= **Lawry's Cornish Giant**), an apple from the Tamar Valley, has very large fruits, which are tall and crowned and have a rounded base. The colouring is spectacular, the apples developing from green but turning yellow with bold, red-pink striping. It is a culinary apple with an acid flavour and soft flesh, and holds its shape well on baking, despite a tendency to purée. It is said to make a very light (ladies') cider.

Duke of Cornwall is a medium to large apple from South of Truro, bearing tallish, rounded, but locular-shaped fruits with pale, blue-green, almost translucent skin that turns golden-yellow and develops a red flush from the stalk end. A late culinary apple keeping until Easter, it has a good, sharp flavour. It is a disease-free, reliable cropper.

Hocking's Green bears apples which are not very inspiring visually, except that they are regularly shaped, clean and shiny green. It produces uniform, medium to large fruits which are round, tallish and clean-cut; when fully ripe, they turn greenish-yellow and greasy. The apples have deepish eyes that tend to be distinctly open. A culinary apple that seems to have originated in Coad's Green, East Cornwall, it is of excellent keeping quality, and has a distinctly tart flavour. A very reliable cropper and as disease-free as they come.

King Byerd is, in my opinion, probably the best of the indigenous culinary apples. It is found right across mid-Cornwall from Looe to Redruth, and produces medium to large, locular, rounded, flattened fruits. The apples are beautiful, initially green, but maturing to yellow overlaid with russet, and flushing a brilliant coral-pink on the exposed side. The flesh is very white and crisp. It is a late-season variety and should not be used until after Christmas – it keeps easily until Easter. A large, spreading tree, it is a regular and prolific cropper. Mary Rich calls it her 'Dutch Old Master painting' apple!

Tregonna King (= **Bacon Apple** or **Lady Bacon**) was distributed by Tregonna Nurseries of Padstow, and is very similar to King of the Pippins. It produces medium to large, round, slightly tall fruits, each with a deep-set eye. These are initially green, but quickly turn yellow with a slight russet and then a characteristic orange base, with a coral-pink flush and stripes. It is chiefly regarded as a culinary variety, but could be eaten after Christmas. It is a very reliable and prolific cropper, common in mid- and North Cornwall.

DESSERT VARIETIES

Ben's Red, in its accepted form, produces small to medium-sized, uniformly round and flattened, shiny red fruits with a distinctive orange-russet overflowing as streaks from the cavity around the stalk. The flesh is bright white and crisp, becoming suffused with pink as it softens and matures. It crops during the second-early season, and forms a small, bushy tree which roots from cuttings and has healthy, vigorous, shiny green foliage. It originated in the Penzance area in 1830. Available nationally, it (and/or very similar seedlings) is still widely seen in Cornwall. The apples are best eaten straight from the tree.

Cornish Gilliflower is one of the great apples when grown from virus-free stock. It is still regarded by the *cognoscenti* as having the best flavour, with a slightly clove fragrance predominating. The fruit is distinct, medium-sized, tall and often lop-sided, with a ridged crown. The skin turns from green to brown and then flushes red with a light russetting. It is a late- to very late-season variety, and should be stood until Christmas to achieve the development of the full flavour and texture. It develops into a large, spreading tree with healthy, shiny foliage. It is tip-bearing, so any pruning should take account of this factor.

Cornish Pine, a name applied to more than one selection, is from the East of the county. It is a mid-season dessert apple with large, tall fruits which develop a yellow ground that becomes almost completely suffused with a dull red flush and some russet. The apples tend to develop soft flesh if left to stand, but have a very distinctive pineapple flavour. The variety is more disease-prone than most, but if grown on a vigorous rootstock and kept fed, it is worth the effort required to grow it successfully.

Devon Crimson Queen (the type known as **Queenie**) is one of the group of apples with dark, purple-red fruit, shiny skin and a distinctive plum-type bloom, typified by Devonshire Quarrenden. A second-early variety, it produces medium- to large-sized, round, flattened fruits, with white flesh which quickly becomes flushed with pink. The apples have a good, sweet, sub-acid flavour and are best eaten from the tree, but will keep in the short term.

Scilly Pearl originated on the Isles of Scilly and is noted here as a whimsy to remind me of boyhood holiday work at Normandy Farm, St Mary's, where, in late August, we scrumped these apples for eating at 'smokoe'. A medium-sized, round, somewhat flattened fruit with an almost translucent, pale green skin and white flesh, it is very easily bruised so has to be eaten from the tree. It has a wonderful, aromatic flavour – especially good for savouring after you have spent a day slaving in the garden!

Sweet Merlin produces small to medium-sized, round, somewhat flattened fruits. These are initially green but quickly turn to a rich golden-yellow, covered with considerable but light russetting. The flavour is sweet and pleasant. It crops in the second-early season and is a reliable and prolific cropper. This variety is commonly found in mid-Cornwall, especially on the Roseland Peninsula.

White Quarentine was introduced commercially by Veitch in the nineteenth century. Once thought to be lost, it is, in fact, still common in mid-Cornwall: only the name had been mislaid. It develops into a medium-sized, compact tree, which produces small to medium-sized, round, somewhat flattened fruits with characteristically long and slender stalks. The skin becomes primrose yellow and develops a streaky russetting down the fruit from the stalk end. The apple crops during the second-early season and the fruit has crisp flesh and a good flavour.

DUAL-PURPOSE VARIETIES

Breadfruit, found in East Cornwall, produces large, tallish, often lop-sided fruit, ridged at the crown. The skin is green, turning to greenish-yellow with a reddish-brown flush over most of the apple, the remainder being striped. The flesh has a sweet, sub-acid flavour reminiscent of strawberries, is very white, and retains its structure on cooking. Mid-season for cooking, it can be eaten until November.

Improved Keswick, presumed to be a seedling of Keswick Codlin, which it resembles, originates from the Tamar Valley. It is a medium-sized, tall, narrow apple with a bright yellow skin, and is ridged at the crown. It has the same green eyelashes as Keswick Codlin. Good for cooking as it retains its structure, it can be eaten after Christmas and has a sub-acid, pleasant flavour. It is a mid- to late-season variety and keeps until March. It crops reliably and prolifically, and suffers little from disease.

Manaccan Primrose has medium to large, regularly round, but very slightly flattened fruits, with green skin which quickly turns to a rich, clear, pale yellow and develops a little flush on the sunny side. It has a crisp flesh with a sharp and tangy flavour in the early season, and matures by late October, when it can be eaten. The yields are reliable. The variety originated in Manaccan but is a seedling series: the plant described is one typical clone.

Snell's White (= **Glass Apple**) is found mostly in South-east Cornwall and bears medium to large-sized, even-shaped, round to tall fruit, ribbed towards the crown. The skin is pale yellow, often spotted with russet, and becomes greasy when mature. The flesh is crisp, white and juicy, with a slightly sweet, acid flavour. It fruits during the second-early to mid-season and is a reliable cropper.

PICKLING VARIETIES

There is a long tradition of pickling apples in Cornwall: they were often eaten as a treat for Sunday tea with bread, cream and honey ('thunder and lightning'). The varieties used were commonly small (one inch in diameter), round, sometimes slightly flattened apples, mostly green-skinned, firm-fleshed, acid in flavour, and with very long, slender stalks. A whole series of seedlings of this description is often referred to as the **Cornish Longstems**, which can be found throughout Cornwall. **Chacewater Longstem** is one particular example which ripens to a yellow skin. The original tree, which still stands, was found in the garden of The Count House of Wheal Busy mine.

Sweet Larks is exceptional for a pickling apple in that it has a sweetish flavour. The skin ripens to yellow and the fruits are larger than normal for the type – up to one and a half inches in diameter. This variety is found West of Truro but chiefly around Hayle, Guildford and Angarrack.

CIDER VARIETIES

Cider production has always been part of the rural cycle in areas where apples are produced in any quantity, and Cornwall is no exception. But not all Cornish cider apple varieties are typical. Cider apples tend to be quite small, and many of the Cornish ones are; but several local varieties, most typically those from the Lerryn and St Veep area, produce fruits of immense size.

Dufflin, a variety from the Truro area, has small to medium-sized fruits with mid-season maturity. It is a full, bitter-sharp type with a high sugar content, and is used widely for blending.

Hamlyn is a bittersweet variety from St Veep, named after the farm where it was collected. It produces medium to large, regular, rounded, slightly flattened fruits with green skin which matures to pale yellow-green. It is a reliable and heavy cropper.

John Broad (= **Captain Broad**), another bittersweet apple, is from the Golant area. The fruits are medium to large, and round to conical in shape. The skin turns from green to yellow and develops a few red stripes and slight russetting.

Lord of the Isles is one of the major varieties from the Lerryn–St Veep–Golant area. It bears very large, good-looking, round, slightly flattened, locular fruit. The green skin develops red-brown flushes and streaks over the whole fruit. The white flesh has a bitter, sharp flavour.

Tan Harvey, a bittersweet apple from the Tamar Valley, has medium-sized, very regular, round, flattened fruits with green skin that turns yellow with a pink flush. It is a reliable, heavy-cropping variety.

PEARS

The varieties of pear available from the nineteenth century were virtually all of French origin, or at least derived from French varieties. When grown in the Cornish climate as free-standing trees, they did not tolerate the soil, the wind, the salt, or the diseases. Perhaps it was for this reason that they did not lend themselves to local selection in the same way as apples: only oddities such as **Swan's Egg** seemed to have the necessary constitution. Indeed, a tree of this variety remains from Heligan's past (left). It had obviously been espaliered on a north-facing wall in the Melon Yard and, in tribute to its powers of survival, it remains untouched, an ungainly specimen growing above the wall and obliging us by fruiting regularly. A few single cordons are being grown on the west-facing wall near the apples, and so far have survived. They are: **Hessle**, **Packham's Triumph**, **Louise Bonne of Jersey** (top right), **William's Bon Chretien**, **Concorde**, **Conference** (above right), **Onward**, **Beurre Hardy** (above, left) and **Doyenne du Comice**. Descriptions of these are available in many modern fruit books. A couple of trees of **Doyenne du Comice** are also now being espaliered on wires down the centre of the Melon Yard.

QUINCE AND MEDLAR

A trawl through an old Cornish orchard will almost invariably reveal at least one medlar tree and one quince. Normally the medlar is the old traditional **Nottingham** variety. The fruits are 'bletted' before they are used. Bletting involves harvesting the fruits when they are still quite hard and flavourless, and then standing them on a tray of clean sand in a dark shed, attic, or room (protected from mice) and leaving them to ripen until they are soft and almost rotten. At this stage the flesh becomes very sweet and highly flavoured, and is regarded as a delicacy by many. The quince is sometimes found to be the old apple-shaped type, but more often is one of the Balkan types (usually **Vranja**), although very occasionally the North American variety **Meeche's Prolific** appears. This last is a particularly distinctive tree, being small and twiggy and producing a heavy crop of relatively small, pear-shaped, golden fruits – a decorative and productive tree for any garden. The fruit of the quince was used to add flavour to apple pies, make quince pies and tarts, or to make quince cheese, among many other lesser uses.

WILD FRUITS

Many of us collect blackberries from the hedgerows in the late Summer, but the seasonal collection and use of other fruits (sweet chestnuts, hazel-nuts and bilberries, for example) has now become a rare occupation. The gathering of fruits from various *Sorbus* species, both to eat as a delicacy and for making jelly, has nearly disappeared, although a selection of rowan called **Edulis**, with particularly large berries suitable for jelly-making, can still be obtained. The fruits of one of the service trees, *Sorbus torminalis*, were collected in times gone by. These were allowed to blet in a similar fashion to medlar fruits and then eaten as a delicacy. These fruits were known as chequers and account for the naming of many public houses, especially in the South of England.

THE SAGA OF THE OTMAST

The story of the otmast is a local twist on this last tradition. In 2001, at a Friends' Evening held at Heligan, one Friend handed us copies of some documents concerning the garden, which she had discovered in the Courtney Library at Truro Museum. One of the subjects of these papers was the collection of a wild fruit known as an 'otmast'. The trees were said to have grown at Heligan, and collection of the fruit in 1912 is mentioned. The fruits were much prized by Squire John Claude (Jack) Tremayne, and were used for 'stuffing cooked pheasants': the writer goes on to say that the fruits were more highly prized than the birds! The trees bearing these fruits were described as being down the 'horse lane from

Peruppa to Heligan House' and 'in the wood below Nancellan Lane End at Temple'. Naturally, our interest was aroused and enquiries were initiated by Peter Stafford, our Managing Director (on the right, hunting the otmast). Initial attempts to identify the trees, their position, and the origins of the name failed. The various stabs at lining up potential subjects included the fruits of *Osmanthus armatus*: the osmanth-otmast phonetic trip was seductive, but the plant was not introduced to cultivation until 1902, and why would it have been planted in the woods and not the garden? Another candidate was the fruit of *Cornus capitata* which was historically a Heligan plant and has edible fruits; but it was grown everywhere around the gardens.

Then, as a result of a note in the Friends' Newsletter, a local lady recognized the name otmast. She recollected that, during the 1940s, she had collected these fruits as a girl, in the company of her father, a boy who was later to become her husband, and her sister, in the woods at Heligan. Her father, Preston Thomas, a renowned Mevagissey sailor, had been a friend of Jack Tremayne. After several exploratory visits to the estate, she and her husband eventually located the tree at Temple, during the Autumn when the fruits were found and allowed for its recognition. The tree itself was in pretty poor and decrepit condition, but fruits were collected from it and sent to Westonbirt Arboretum, whose staff tentatively identified them as 'French Hales' (*Sorbus devoniensis*). Bean, in his *Trees and Shrubs Hardy in the British Isles*, notes that the fruits had been known to be sold in Barnstaple market. *Sorbus devoniensis* is one of several apomictic species of the whitebeam section of the genus. All of these species are usually of very local distribution in the UK. They are probably all of hybrid origin, and are part of the service tree complex. This species, as its name implies, is localized in Devon and East Cornwall.

But what of the name otmast? Various semi-logical lines of thought eventually suggested that 'ot' could be either 'belonging to a place' (as in 'Zealot' or 'Cypriot') or, more usefully, to describe something small (as in 'ballot'). 'Mast' is, of course, in reasonably common use to denote fruit – as in beech mast. All this adds up to a possible concocted name describing 'small fruit'.

CHAPTER 6
THE PEACH HOUSE AND ITS CROPPING

The lean-to greenhouse in the Walled Garden, designed for the cultivation of peaches and nectarines, was originally built in about 1880. Although it has been restored to its original condition, the ground-plan of the garden seems to suggest that it may not have been the first glasshouse to be built on this particular site. Situated in the Walled Garden for maximum protection from the elements, it is oriented south-south-west in order to gain the greatest benefit from the sun during the Spring. This advantageous situation has been achieved by the eccentric design of the ground-plan of this garden and the particular construction of the building, a notable characteristic of which is the size of the glazing panes. By the 1880s, the quality of glassmaking had improved to the extent that large, flat pieces of glass could be made, and so larger (traditionally 14 ins.-wide) panes could be used for glazing. This significantly reduced the number of glazing bars required, so improving light transmission. It was also no longer necessary to cut the tops and bottoms of the panes in the 'beaver-tail' fashion, as the glazing bars did not need to be light, fragile, and hence susceptible to wet and then rot, and the panes were therefore cut straight across. The Peach House subtends a redbrick wall and is 82 ft. long. The height to the ridge-board is 12 ft. 6 ins.; the height of the front wall 24 ins., and the width of the house from front to back 12 ft. 3 ins. This creates a 40° pitch of the roof, significant insofar as the angle is set to maximize radiation input during the Spring. At this time the angle of insolation achieves highest straight-through penetration (rather than losing some through reflection).

Maximizing solar gain is vital, as the Peach House has no other form of heating: the construction and position of the house ensure that it accumulates heat rapidly, even when the sun appears only for short periods in the day. The temperature inside the greenhouse is managed by opening or closing the boxed ventilation ducts along the two-foot-high brick wall, which supports the roof at the front, in conjunction with the roof vents – sliding lights which can be hauled up or down to open or close them. Temperature management in this house can therefore be a logistical nightmare in the variable climate of Cornwall, where,

The Peach House: derelict (top); restored (middle); in fruit (bottom)

even in the Summer, cloud-banks occur irregularly and for indeterminate periods of time. Labour is no longer so readily available or so cheap that staff can be on hand continually to ventilate the Peach House as required; however, by dint of careful observation and efficient deployment of our brave, observant and multi-skilled workforce, the environment is managed within acceptable limits.

During the Autumn and early winter months, both top and bottom vents and the doors are kept fully open to provide maximum air circulation and keep the temperature within the house as low as possible. Such a reduction in temperature is required by the deciduous fruit trees to cause the onset of dormancy and the subsequent vernalization of the buds, and ensures that an even bud-break occurs in the Spring as temperatures rise again. (The mild winters experienced in Cornwall make for a potential problem with this process, but, in practice, these particular species have a relatively high chilling threshold, and therefore a low chilling requirement, so lowering the temperature in the house sufficiently is not difficult.) When the trees have had adequate exposure to cold, the house is closed up in order to encourage bud-break and flowering. Peaches have highly decorative, large, pink flowers, which appear before

Johanna with a trug of peaches, outside the restored Peach House (top); the same, derelict (above)

the leaves, and the Peach House is a beautiful sight in this season. Spring and summer temperatures are then regulated by judicious ventilation, and shading can also be applied in high Summer if necessary. The other crucial feature is the watering regime: dry conditions are maintained in the Winter, watering being carried out during the relevant growth periods in the Summer, especially at the time when the fruit is swelling.

Because these trees flower early in the Spring (see following page) when the house may often be closed up, artificial pollination of the flowers should be carried out in order to achieve a good level of fertilization. It is unlikely that there will be enough insects about to ensure natural pollination of a sufficient magnitude. Hand pollination

can be achieved by using the proverbial rabbit's tail, or an artist's paintbrush. However, success is dependent on an ability to recognize when the anthers dehisce and liberate pollen, and when the stigmas are receptive. After fruit-set is apparent, the next phase is 'stoning' – the stage when the peaches develop stones and could make fruits. When this stage has been reached, the fruits are thinned out. There are then two options to follow: you can either pursue a programme of management (watering, feeding and pruning) dictated by commonsense, or choose a contemporaneous volume and try to follow the guiding hand!

One of the considerable advantages of growing these species under glass is that they do not suffer from the fungal scourge of this group of stone fruits, peach leaf curl (*Taphrina deformans*). However, they do tend to be subject to infestation by red spider mite and aphids. The former pest can be controlled by maintaining high humidity, to keep populations to a minimum, and using biological methods. Aphids are best dealt with by using soft soap, biological controls, or a targeted insecticide. Our preferred solution for both is to use biological techniques.

The restored Peach House is used principally for the production of peaches and nectarines, but is also home to a pineapple guava, the occasional passion fruit and a decorative climbing plant from Australia, *Hardenbergia violacea*.

PEACHES AND NECTARINES

It is as well to point out, early on, that the nectarine is nothing more than a smooth-skinned variant of the peach. Both peaches and nectarines are inherently strong-growing subjects and are potentially gross feeders. They succeed best in a fertile soil with good water-holding capacity, but which is nevertheless well drained. Like apricots, they perform most satisfactorily in alkaline soil conditions, so attention should be paid to the lime status. At Heligan, the borders for peaches and nectarines were double-dug, with the incorporation of large quantities of well-rotted manure, prior to planting. Balanced fertilizers are applied annually. In Cornwall, peaches and nectarines could be grown on a well-sheltered, sunny, south-facing wall, or even as free-standing trees; but, for reliable and consist-ent performance, they are best managed in the advantageous environment of an unheated greenhouse. Our trees are grown both on the back wall of the lean-to house and at the front – the latter are trained against and under the slope of the roof. Training under the glass has been made possible by the reinstatement of the wiring configuration, using the traditional, galvanized, nine-inch-long eye-bolts, screwed into the roof joists at 12-ins. intervals and then transversely threading and tensioning the wires, anchored on end plates, through these. This allows the foliage to be carried at 12 ins. below the glass. Ideally, the trees would be planted at 15-ft. intervals along the length of the house (both front and back) at about four

Young fan-trained peach tree

inches from the wall, meaning that ten trees could be planted, but the passion fruit and the pineapple guava complicate the issue and reduce this potential.

As strong-growing subjects, peaches must be constrained by the use of a dwarfing rootstock (**St Julien A**) and, if required, by root pruning. Despite the fact that the present stock, our original planting, is producing a significant crop each year, the trees have fared no better than most of the other fan-trained fruit, and we are in the process of replanting for the long term. The back wall has already been replanted, and trees against the front wall will be replaced over the next few years.

VARIETIES

Our selections from the available period-correct varieties of peach and nectarine, *Prunus persica*, are made chiefly on the basis of the need for an early season of cropping, so that any down-turn in late-season weather does not cause a problem with maturing the crop. We have enjoyed eating the fruits of the varieties listed below, which have, in general, cropped prolifically. One of the delights of our job is to have the opportunity to eat a fully ripe peach picked directly from the tree: the sheer decadence of having the juice drip down your chin and stain your tie or your waistcoat has to be experienced! Ripe peaches of this type and vintage are notoriously soft, melting and juicy, and bruise very easily: picking them without damaging the fruit is an art form in itself, and carrying them anywhere is another exercise in care and restraint – hence the need to eat them *in situ*. This type of peach should not be confused with the firm, orange-fleshed varieties of modern commerce.

PEACH

Amsden June, one of the earliest-season peaches, is of American origin and was introduced in 1868. The fruits are of medium size, maturing in mid-July. They are irregularly round with a wide, deep suture, greenish-white skin with an extensive red flush, and greenish-white, melting flesh with a good flavour.

Duke of York was raised by Messrs Rivers and introduced in 1902. It is an early variety, its large, round fruits, slightly flattened across the shallow suture, maturing in mid-July. The skin is pale with extensive crimson colouring right around the fruit, and the flesh is a pale greenish-yellow, melting, with a sweet but tart edge to its flavour: a refreshing peach.

Peregrine (see chapter opening), again raised by Messrs Rivers and introduced in 1906, is a prolific mid-

Peaches: Duke of York (top); Peregrine (middle); Rochester (bottom)

season variety with fairly large fruits maturing in early August. These are round with a deep suture, and pale yellowish-white skin almost completely covered in a deep, brilliant crimson-red flush. The flesh is yellowish-white, firm, juicy and has a fine flavour. Peregrine is still the standard for this type of peach.

Rochester is of American origin and was introduced to the UK in 1912. It is a mid-season variety with large fruits that mature in early to mid-August. A prolific cropper, this variety produces round peaches with a prominent suture, a pale skin with an orange-red flush, and yellow flesh.

NECTARINE

Early Rivers (= **John Rivers**) is a very early-season variety, cropping three weeks before Lord Napier, in early July. It was raised and introduced in 1893 by T.F. Rivers. The fruits are large, round and usually somewhat flattened across the broad, shallow suture. The skin is greenish-yellow, almost completely covered in a dark, striped, brilliant scarlet flush. A prolific cropper, it produces peaches with pale yellow, very tender and juicy flesh, which has a rich flavour.

Elruge is an old, prolific, mid-season variety of uncertain origin, reputed to be the hardiest nectarine. Maturing towards the end of August, the fruits are round with a tendency to be elongated, have a shallow suture and pale greenish-white skin with a dull purplish-red flush. The melting, greenish-white flesh has a red stain at the stone and a delicious perfumed flavour.

Lord Napier, a second-early variety, raised by Thomas Rivers and introduced in 1869, has large, oval fruits which taper to the stem and mature in late July or early August. The pale yellow skin is almost completely covered in a brownish-crimson flush; the flesh is a very pale greenish-white, firm, melting and with a rich and refreshing flavour. This variety is a prolific cropper and was the standard for nectarines of pre-First World War vintage.

OTHER GLASSHOUSE FRUITS

The Peach House also contains a few other plants, which, for one reason or another, simply satisfy somebody's personal whimsy – in this case mine!

PASSION FRUITS

Although the edible passion fruit, *Passiflora edulis*, usually crops quite reasonably on an outside wall in Cornwall, it is more reliable and more prolific when grown in a cold greenhouse. The passion flowers are vigorous, semi-evergreen, climbing plants and, once established, produce several stems of at least 30 ft. in length. The Giant Granadilla, *P. quadrangularis*, and the Banana passion fruit, *P. mollissima*, both of which have beautiful flowers and crop prolifically, have been

tried and discarded because they have proved to be too vigorous: we had difficulty in preventing them from completely overwhelming the whole house. One plant of *P. edulis* **Crackerjack** (above, fruit and right, flower) is now cultivated in the Peach House. It is planted in the border under the back wall and is currently allowed to spread about 25 ft. The plant is cut back to an upright stem which is held to a cane, and the side shoots, which are produced annually, are then tied into the horizontal wires and stopped when they have reached the allotted distance. Sub-laterals are pruned back as necessary, in order to keep the plant under control. Flowering is normally prolific, and fruit production extravagant from late August onwards. In late Autumn the shoots are cut back to the main upright and the site is cleaned up. The annual sequence then continues.

PINEAPPLE GUAVA

The pineapple guava, *Feijoa sellowiana* (right), is not seen very often as it will only succeed outside in Cornwall on a well-drained, dry, sheltered, frost-free site. It is grown here at Heligan on the back wall of the Peach House, as a fan-trained specimen. Although I have never seen this done with this plant before, the idea has worked: the plant responds well to pruning and tying in. This densely shrubby plant, with grey-green leaves, is a native of Southern Brazil and Uruguay, but has found its way around the world to various Mediterranean climate niches. If for nothing else, it warrants a place on the basis of its extremely decorative flowers, which are sweet and edible and make an interesting, unusual addition to fruit salads. The plant is cultivated commercially in New Zealand for its fruit, the pineapple

guava. Fruits have sometimes been produced in the Cornish climate, but this is only a realistic possibility with the protection of, at least, an unheated greenhouse. Our specimen, **Apollo**, is one of the less vigorous, commercially cultivated varieties from New Zealand. Self-fertile, it flowers well and occasionally fruits – if enough flowers escape being consumed and are left to permit pollination.

HARDENBERGIA

Hardenbergia violacea (left) is a vigorous and densely branching, climbing, leguminous plant from Australia. For most of the year a specimen grows quietly in the southern corner of the Peach House. After a severe early spring haircut, it proceeds to develop determinedly but unobtrusively during the course of the Summer, producing an intertwining mass of fine stems that fills the end of the house. It is semi-deciduous, but develops its lanceolate leaves in dense profusion in the early Winter and begins to flower in January. The flowers are produced as small panicles of well-defined, pea-type blossoms with purple standards and keels and yellow wings. These are so numerous that no-one who sees it, especially caught in the rays of the winter sun, can but have their spirits uplifted, in the middle of this dreary part of the year. It is our reminder that a new season is with us, and serves to warn us all that the intensive effort of the early season is about to overtake us: it has no other productive purpose.

During the Summer, any vacant space along the back border tended to be used by Johanna for growing some of her many varieties of tomato.

CHAPTER 7
GRAPES AND THE PAXTON HOUSE

To become a head gardener was one of the few avenues open to an intelligent country boy, to achieve a status well above his station. Joseph Paxton was one such example and he excelled in his career, rising through the ranks of the gardening profession and eventually moving from the position of Head Gardener at Chatsworth to become designer of the Crystal Palace, business entrepreneur, Member of Parliament and knight of the realm. The Paxton greenhouse at Heligan is one of the few surviving examples of the thousands manufactured in the mid-1800s by Paxton and his business partner, in the course of one of his many commercial ventures. His concept was to design a cheap, mass-produced, transportable greenhouse, which could be erected from units that were easy to make and assemble. This idea was to provide the middle classes with the opportunity to own greenhouses, which, until that time, had been the prerogative of the rich.

Paxton's greenhouse was among the original flat-pack concepts, the forerunner of much of the domestic furniture and building packages of today, and was delivered by the new-fangled railway. The structure was based on a unit 16 ft. long by four feet wide. Each unit carried four glazing bars reinforced with metal cross-members, and five runs of glass – the production of large sheets of plate glass did not occur until later in the century. The wooden glazing bars were lightweight and would therefore rot quickly if they remained damp, so the glass was cut to a curved, 'beaver-tail' shape, which caused rainwater to drain down the middle of the run of panes and away from the glazing bars: this was, by then, a traditional and well-known technique. A number of these units could be made into a greenhouse, either as a lean-to construction or as a span house depending on one's particular needs, using the various metal supports provided. Two hinged windows that fitted the length of these units provided means for ventilation and were attached to a metal linkage, which allowed them to be opened together or independently. The spacing of the units to receive the windows was achieved by the use of a bracing and spacing bracket, also thoughtfully provided. All of these pieces of metal were recovered from the debris in the semi-collapsed Paxton House at Heligan during the process of recovery and restoration in 1993–94, and were sand-blasted, painted and re-used.

It was the remains of the Paxton House that originally enchanted Tim Smit and inspired him to undertake the rescue of these gardens. The Heligan Paxton House is a lean-to construction, built against part of the south-facing wall of the Walled Garden. The structure consists of eight basic glazed units, with a window vent between each. The units stand on a plinth attached to the top of a low, brick front wall, which contains arches, presumably made for grape cultivation. This wall could well be of an earlier vintage than the Paxton greenhouse, and may simply have been adapted by the Head Gardener when the superstructure was upgraded. The pillars are of brick (about one foot wide and four feet apart) with a thick slate lintel above each and then four courses of brick right along the length, capped with the plinth. This gives an overall height of two feet. The house is divided into two equal sections, each about 18 ft. long, by a glass partition and connecting door. Originally it was heated: as technology advanced, so the heating system was upgraded. The last system to be installed used cast-iron pipes, four inches in diameter, which carried hot water as part of a conventional gravity circulation system. Pipes front the border under the front wall, and another set is sunk in a trench in the path and covered with a cast-iron grille (see previous page). There is no permanent heating in the house now: the installation cost is prohibitive for a system that would be used only for the short ripening period in the Autumn.

The Paxton House: Charles excavating outside (left); inside, derelict, 1993 (top); restored and planted, 1995 (above)

The Paxton House in the Flower Garden, restored

DESSERT GRAPES

Grapes are a productive and relatively easy crop to grow, but even in the far South-west of England it is a safer bet to grow them in a cold greenhouse than outdoors, if a reasonable crop of dessert-quality fruit is required. A long season of cropping can be achieved if several varieties are grown in the sequence of their season of maturity. The late-season varieties almost certainly need additional heat right at the end of the season to produce fruit of the very best flavour. The vine is a vigorous, deciduous, climbing plant, which requires substantial feeding to allow it to grow well, but also rigorous pruning to control its vigour and enhance productivity. Several Victorian and modern books concentrating on vine-growing are listed in the Bibliography, and reference should be made to them if strict adherence to successful practice is to be achieved.

The Heligan vines were planted against the front wall of the greenhouse in the Winter of 1995–96, and trained as single-stem cordons under the glass, by tying them in and under the horizontal wires. They are planted three feet apart, so the two sections of the house have room for six vines each. The earliest-fruiting variety is planted at the coldest end (i.e. alongside the eastern outer side wall),

and the remaining varieties are planted in order of maturity, with the latest ripening in the warmest position, alongside the wall shared with the Citrus House. This arrangement produces a long season of cropping. The roof of the house has been wired along its length at intervals of 12 ins., using nine-inch-long, galvanized eye-bolts to hold and align the wire. This places the wire, and therefore the blanket of foliage, at 12 ins. below the glass. The wires are strained from anchor plates of drilled angle iron, fixed to the end walls.

The annual sequence of operations in the production of a crop of grapes is probably most easily described by starting in the Winter. The major pruning of the plant takes place at this time, as soon as the last bunches have been harvested and the leaves have abscissed. All the side shoots are cut right back to the main, single-cordon stem. This main stem is then cleaned up by removing the fibrous bark tissue which develops during the year – a tedious task but one necessary to expose any scale insects remaining on the bark surface. These are controlled by painting the whole stem with tar oil or similar. All, repeat *all*, the debris in the house is cleared out, and the soil surface lightly cultivated. After pruning and treatment, the cordon stems are released from their ties and lowered to a horizontal position for the duration of the Winter. This allows the stem to readjust its hormonal balance and minimizes the effect of apical dominance, a naturally occurring sequence in which the top bud breaks first, with the remaining buds breaking successively down to the base of the stem. The lowering of the stems overcomes this effect and allows all the buds to break at the same time in the Spring. This even bud-break is also enhanced by keeping the house as cold as possible during the Winter, so that deep vernalization of the buds occurs: if the buds do not become fully dormant, bud-break in the Spring will be erratic, eccentric and late.

Due to the amount of stem and foliage that they produce in a season, vines are gross feeders, and therefore the soil nutrient reserves must be replenished for the new season's growth. The time to feed vines is the Spring, just before the buds begin to break. Our crop is mulched at the same time with well-rotted manure. The season can be advanced by boarding up the arches of the house, thus closing it and creating a warmer environment, which encourages the buds to break. As the buds break and the lateral stems begin to develop, they are thinned to one from each node to each side of the stem, and are tied to the horizontal wires under the glass as they grow, for support. Flowers appear soon and, once pollination has occurred, the lateral stems can be stopped by cutting back to two leaves beyond the potential bunch. If there is no flower they are cut back to five leaves. This all sounds rather drastic, but it is important not to allow the foliage to become overcrowded. After fruit-set, the density of production can be assessed and, if necessary, the number of bunches reduced. As soon as the bunches have

developed individual grapes of a size sufficient to be handled, the number of berries in the bunches can be thinned in order to develop both good size grapes and symmetrical bunches (left, tended by Paul Haywood).

The most likely problem to be encountered during the season is the development of mildew, which, in the worst instances, can devastate both leaves and fruit. Traditionally, this was controlled by the use of Bordeaux Mixture, but today there are a number of targeted fungicides on the market. However, the incidence of mildew is normally low if a dank, cold atmosphere is avoided. Among the insect pests most likely to cause infestations are red spider mite, aphid, scale insect and mealy bug – all of which, once seen, should be treated with the relevant insecticide or biological predator without delay.

STORING THE FRUIT

Bunches of grapes were stored in special, purpose-designed and -manufactured glass bottles (above). We were lucky enough to obtain a crate of these in unused condition, complete with a piece of charcoal in each bottle to keep the water 'sweet'. When mature, the bunches were cut with a good length of stem that could be inserted into the neck of the bottle, which was kept topped up with water and sat on its side on a rack or shelf in the Fruit Room. This allowed the bunches of grapes to hang down freely and, with skill, they could be kept for several weeks.

VARIETIES

The varieties of grape grown at Heligan are described here in order of their maturity. At the moment we do not grow any vines out-of-doors. There are three groups of vine:

Sweetwater These generally tend to crop during the early to mid-season, and have grapes with thin skins and a sweet, juicy flesh.

Muscat These mature principally during the mid-season. They have a distinctive musky flavour and, in this country, require warmth in the Autumn to develop the flavour fully. The skins are substantial without being thick.

Vinous These ripen late in the season, and almost all require heat to finish them to full flavour. The grapes are generally thick-skinned with firm, juicy flesh. They are capable of being stored for up to several months in suitable conditions.

Paxton House number 1 contains:

Royal Muscadine, a very old, white sweetwater variety, probably of Medieval origin, known more widely in Europe by its French name, *Chasselas Dorée*. It is one of the first to mature fruit in the early season. The grapes are small, round and pale yellow with a golden tinge, and have a firm, juicy flesh with a sweet, rich flavour for which the variety is highly esteemed.

Foster's Seedling, a white sweetwater variety of English origin, made *c.* 1836 and introduced to commerce in 1860. It is one of the earliest varieties to mature and produces medium-sized, more or less oval grapes of a pale greenish-yellow colour. These have a soft, melting flesh and a fine sweet flavour.

Chasselas Rose, an old, grizzly (pink) sweetwater variety long grown in this country because of its reliability in cropping, producing small, round grapes of a very distinctive light rose colour, in the early season. They have a juicy, tender flesh with a sweet, pleasant flavour. The bunches tend to be elongated with a distinct shoulder.

Buckland Sweetwater, a white sweetwater variety of English origin, introduced into commercial circulation *c.* 1830. It is early-season in maturity, and produces medium to large, round, pale greenish-yellow grapes. The flesh is soft and very juicy, with a light, sweet, pleasant flavour. The bunches are large and stout and have a strong shoulder.

Madresfield Court, a black muscat variety, of which we have two vines. Of English origin, it was introduced *c.* 1870 and is an early- to mid-season variety. The grapes are long, oval and distinctly flattened at the distal end. The flesh is softish and juicy, with a sweet and slightly muscat flavour. The bunches are long with sloping shoulders.

Paxton House number 2 is home to:

Lady Hutt, a fairly modern, white, sweetwater, mid-season variety of English origin, introduced in 1899. The grapes are medium-sized, round, and ripen to a clear, pale yellow. The flesh is firm and juicy, with a sweet, subtle flavour.

Muscat Hamburg, an old, black muscat, mid-season variety of uncertain origin, but probably from the Middle East. The grapes are oval to round with a prominent white bloom. The flesh is firm and sweet and has a very strong muscat flavour. The bunches are loose and long, with a strongly sloping shoulder.

Black Hamburg – of which we have two vines – probably the best-known greenhouse grape. This variety of the plant, famous for its size and longevity, grows at Hampton Court Palace. An old, black sweetwater variety, it matures in the mid- to late season. The grapes are large, roundish, have a noticeable bluish bloom, and are produced in big bunches with a very distinct shoulder. The flesh is firm and juicy, with a sweet, mild flavour.

Muscat of Alexandria, a very old and well-known white muscat variety from Southern Europe – one of the great dessert grapes. It matures in the late season, and for the development of its full flavour probably needs heat to finish it off. The grapes are large, long and oval in shape, turning from a pale green to a pale straw yellow at full ripeness. The flesh is soft and juicy, with a sweet but rich muscat flavour. The bunches tend to be long and straggly with sloping shoulders.

Gros Colman, a very old, black, vinous variety, probably originating from the Caucasus. It is one of the latest varieties to be grown successfully in this country, and certainly needs heat to finish and develop the flavour of the fruit. It was the preferred variety for the Christmas table and could be stored well into the New Year in a vine bottle in the cellar. The grapes are very large, round and black, with a subtle purple bloom and a thick skin. The flesh is soft and tender, with a sweet, wine-like flavour. The bunches tend to be uneven all round.

Since I wrote these notes, the vinery has suffered 'the slings and arrows of outrageous fortune', in the form of an extremely unusual disease – *Eutypa*. This causes all the stems beyond the point of infection to die, so when infection occurs at about ground level the results are spectacularly disappointing: all of this when we had just got the plants to a mature size and good cropping level (about eight years old). If the infected tissue is cut out we can, apparently, run up another stem – small consolation! During the Winter of 2002–03 it was decided that such a process was too hit and miss, as infection might well come back to haunt us. We therefore got rid of all the plants and removed all the soil in the Paxton House to a good three feet in depth (thanks to Emiliano Sanchez). The houses were then washed down and sterilized, and the rooting area filled with fresh soil. New plants of the same varieties were obtained and have been planted. These are now in the process of being trained into the required condition.

The back wall of the Paxton House carries some shelving, which, together with the floor, provides a home to plants – mostly half-hardy bulbous subjects – which do not conflict with the use of the house as a vinery.

FIGS

A luxury fruit crop that has been grown in the UK for centuries by those with the resources necessary to achieve success, figs were probably introduced during the Roman occupation and have certainly been in continuous cultivation since the Medieval period. The acme of their cultivation was probably achieved during the second half of the nineteenth century when they were cultivated extensively in the glasshouses and walled gardens of the landed and moneyed classes, and were included in the productive garden schedule of any self-respecting head gardener. The production of a crop of figs can still be a reasonably successful enterprise in any home garden if the relatively simple needs and processes of the crop are understood. The fresh fig may be an acquired taste; but once a crop has been produced and ripened on the tree, the flavour and texture will probably make it a 'must have'. It is currently a fashionable fruit (as an imported commodity), and is used regularly in dessert recipes by 'celebrity chefs'.

The fig is a vigorous, extraordinarily tenacious and long-lived tree and, in the process of its cultivation, will put up with what appears to be draconian treatment. If allowed unrestricted growing conditions and a reasonably fertile soil it can develop into a large, bushy tree, up to 15 or 20 ft. in height and spread and, once fully grown, it crops prolifically.

Fruit production in the UK depends on proper 'ripening' of the current season's shoots: the shoot must become mature and woody right to the tip, otherwise frost will quickly destroy the tissues. Although the origins of the fig are obscure, it is most likely to have originated in Mesopotamia. This implies the need for a sunny position and hence, in most parts of the country, training or planting against a south-facing wall. In Cornwall we are fortunate that we can grow and crop figs out-of-doors and without protection relatively easily. The other crucial feature of cultivation is to restrict root growth dramatically so that shoot growth is also restricted and energy is channelled into the setting of fruit buds. This treatment constrains the development of the tree and keeps it within manageable proportions. If the fig is to be planted against a wall it will require about a 15-ft. run and a traditional, sealed brick bed of up to two cubic yards' capacity. This needs to be constructed with a good layer of drainage in the base; but there should be no avenue for the roots to escape out of this constraint and, *de facto*, no drainage outlet. Crop management does mean, therefore, that considerable attention has to be paid to watering in the summer. The fig fruits on the

previous year's wood, having set the fruit by the first Autumn. This fruit-set can be enhanced by stopping the shoots in early Autumn, a process that involves cutting back the shoots to the fifth or sixth leaf. The fruits are about the size of a pea at this stage, but survive the Winter satisfactorily. Pruning requires the removal of the fruiting shoot in Winter after fruiting and the thinning of the shoots in Summer, to create an acceptable structure for fruit production.

We have been able to obtain a good range of varieties, selected from those that would have been available in the nineteenth century. These were obtained from Reads of Norfolk, who hold the National Collection of fig varieties. Although we have planted a couple against a wall in the Reserve Garden, the rest have been planted and established in wooden half-barrels of four and a half gallons' capacity. These stand outside on a gravel bed in the walled garden, under the south wall. This permits the barrels to be tipped up each year, quite easily, and the roots which have emerged can be pruned back. Now, after three years of judicious pruning, we have established plants with a suitable framework for fruit production and are beginning to reap the benefits. However, figs are tenacious plants: one on the south-facing wall of the Walled Garden, probably Brown Turkey, has survived the loss of its greenhouse, broken out of its brick box and run wild, yet still produces large crops of edible figs every year (see page 113, harvested by John Nelson). It has been persuaded, year by year, to take its proper place on the wall and relinquish its domination of valuable space for growing other crops (above). It was finally constrained to its original place in 2003, but still has a free run for its roots!

VARIETIES

Varieties grown at Heligan are (opposite):

Angelique, a mid-season variety, which needs wall protection. The fruit is medium-sized and roundish, the skin yellow with white dots. The flesh is white tinged with pink, and has a sweet flavour.

Black Ischia, a mid-season variety with hardy, medium-sized fruit shaped like an inverted cone with both ends flattened. It has purplish-black skin and crimson flesh which is sweet and juicy.

and the remaining varieties are planted in order of maturity, with the latest ripening in the warmest position, alongside the wall shared with the Citrus House. This arrangement produces a long season of cropping. The roof of the house has been wired along its length at intervals of 12 ins., using nine-inch-long, galvanized eye-bolts to hold and align the wire. This places the wire, and therefore the blanket of foliage, at 12 ins. below the glass. The wires are strained from anchor plates of drilled angle iron, fixed to the end walls.

The annual sequence of operations in the production of a crop of grapes is probably most easily described by starting in the Winter. The major pruning of the plant takes place at this time, as soon as the last bunches have been harvested and the leaves have abscissed. All the side shoots are cut right back to the main, single-cordon stem. This main stem is then cleaned up by removing the fibrous bark tissue which develops during the year – a tedious task but one necessary to expose any scale insects remaining on the bark surface. These are controlled by painting the whole stem with tar oil or similar. All, repeat *all*, the debris in the house is cleared out, and the soil surface lightly cultivated. After pruning and treatment, the cordon stems are released from their ties and lowered to a horizontal position for the duration of the Winter. This allows the stem to readjust its hormonal balance and minimizes the effect of apical dominance, a naturally occurring sequence in which the top bud breaks first, with the remaining buds breaking successively down to the base of the stem. The lowering of the stems overcomes this effect and allows all the buds to break at the same time in the Spring. This even bud-break is also enhanced by keeping the house as cold as possible during the Winter, so that deep vernalization of the buds occurs: if the buds do not become fully dormant, bud-break in the Spring will be erratic, eccentric and late.

Due to the amount of stem and foliage that they produce in a season, vines are gross feeders, and therefore the soil nutrient reserves must be replenished for the new season's growth. The time to feed vines is the Spring, just before the buds begin to break. Our crop is mulched at the same time with well-rotted manure. The season can be advanced by boarding up the arches of the house, thus closing it and creating a warmer environment, which encourages the buds to break. As the buds break and the lateral stems begin to develop, they are thinned to one from each node to each side of the stem, and are tied to the horizontal wires under the glass as they grow, for support. Flowers appear soon and, once pollination has occurred, the lateral stems can be stopped by cutting back to two leaves beyond the potential bunch. If there is no flower they are cut back to five leaves. This all sounds rather drastic, but it is important not to allow the foliage to become overcrowded. After fruit-set, the density of production can be assessed and, if necessary, the number of bunches reduced. As soon as the bunches have

developed individual grapes of a size sufficient to be handled, the number of berries in the bunches can be thinned in order to develop both good size grapes and symmetrical bunches (left, tended by Paul Haywood).

The most likely problem to be encountered during the season is the development of mildew, which, in the worst instances, can devastate both leaves and fruit. Traditionally, this was controlled by the use of Bordeaux Mixture, but today there are a number of targeted fungicides on the market. However, the incidence of mildew is normally low if a dank, cold atmosphere is avoided. Among the insect pests most likely to cause infestations are red spider mite, aphid, scale insect and mealy bug – all of which, once seen, should be treated with the relevant insecticide or biological predator without delay.

STORING THE FRUIT

Bunches of grapes were stored in special, purpose-designed and -manufactured glass bottles (above). We were lucky enough to obtain a crate of these in unused condition, complete with a piece of charcoal in each bottle to keep the water 'sweet'. When mature, the bunches were cut with a good length of stem that could be inserted into the neck of the bottle, which was kept topped up with water and sat on its side on a rack or shelf in the Fruit Room. This allowed the bunches of grapes to hang down freely and, with skill, they could be kept for several weeks.

VARIETIES

The varieties of grape grown at Heligan are described here in order of their maturity. At the moment we do not grow any vines out-of-doors. There are three groups of vine:

Sweetwater These generally tend to crop during the early to mid-season, and have grapes with thin skins and a sweet, juicy flesh.

Muscat These mature principally during the mid-season. They have a distinctive musky flavour and, in this country, require warmth in the Autumn to develop the flavour fully. The skins are substantial without being thick.

Vinous These ripen late in the season, and almost all require heat to finish them to full flavour. The grapes are generally thick-skinned with firm, juicy flesh. They are capable of being stored for up to several months in suitable conditions.

Paxton House number 1 contains:

Royal Muscadine, a very old, white sweetwater variety, probably of Medieval origin, known more widely in Europe by its French name, *Chasselas Dorée*. It is one of the first to mature fruit in the early season. The grapes are small, round and pale yellow with a golden tinge, and have a firm, juicy flesh with a sweet, rich flavour for which the variety is highly esteemed.

Foster's Seedling, a white sweetwater variety of English origin, made *c.* 1836 and introduced to commerce in 1860. It is one of the earliest varieties to mature and produces medium-sized, more or less oval grapes of a pale greenish-yellow colour. These have a soft, melting flesh and a fine sweet flavour.

Chasselas Rose, an old, grizzly (pink) sweetwater variety long grown in this country because of its reliability in cropping, producing small, round grapes of a very distinctive light rose colour, in the early season. They have a juicy, tender flesh with a sweet, pleasant flavour. The bunches tend to be elongated with a distinct shoulder.

Buckland Sweetwater, a white sweetwater variety of English origin, introduced into commercial circulation *c.* 1830. It is early-season in maturity, and produces medium to large, round, pale greenish-yellow grapes. The flesh is soft and very juicy, with a light, sweet, pleasant flavour. The bunches are large and stout and have a strong shoulder.

Madresfield Court, a black muscat variety, of which we have two vines. Of English origin, it was introduced *c.* 1870 and is an early- to mid-season variety. The grapes are long, oval and distinctly flattened at the distal end. The flesh is softish and juicy, with a sweet and slightly muscat flavour. The bunches are long with sloping shoulders.

Paxton House number 2 is home to:

Lady Hutt, a fairly modern, white, sweetwater, mid-season variety of English origin, introduced in 1899. The grapes are medium-sized, round, and ripen to a clear, pale yellow. The flesh is firm and juicy, with a sweet, subtle flavour.

Muscat Hamburg, an old, black muscat, mid-season variety of uncertain origin, but probably from the Middle East. The grapes are oval to round with a prominent white bloom. The flesh is firm and sweet and has a very strong muscat flavour. The bunches are loose and long, with a strongly sloping shoulder.

Black Hamburg – of which we have two vines – probably the best-known greenhouse grape. This variety of the plant, famous for its size and longevity, grows at Hampton Court Palace. An old, black sweetwater variety, it matures in the mid- to late season. The grapes are large, roundish, have a noticeable bluish bloom, and are produced in big bunches with a very distinct shoulder. The flesh is firm and juicy, with a sweet, mild flavour.

Muscat of Alexandria, a very old and well-known white muscat variety from Southern Europe – one of the great dessert grapes. It matures in the late season, and for the development of its full flavour probably needs heat to finish it off. The grapes are large, long and oval in shape, turning from a pale green to a pale straw yellow at full ripeness. The flesh is soft and juicy, with a sweet but rich muscat flavour. The bunches tend to be long and straggly with sloping shoulders.

Gros Colman, a very old, black, vinous variety, probably originating from the Caucasus. It is one of the latest varieties to be grown successfully in this country, and certainly needs heat to finish and develop the flavour of the fruit. It was the preferred variety for the Christmas table and could be stored well into the New Year in a vine bottle in the cellar. The grapes are very large, round and black, with a subtle purple bloom and a thick skin. The flesh is soft and tender, with a sweet, wine-like flavour. The bunches tend to be uneven all round.

Since I wrote these notes, the vinery has suffered 'the slings and arrows of outrageous fortune', in the form of an extremely unusual disease – *Eutypa*. This causes all the stems beyond the point of infection to die, so when infection occurs at about ground level the results are spectacularly disappointing: all of this when we had just got the plants to a mature size and good cropping level (about eight years old). If the infected tissue is cut out we can, apparently, run up another stem – small consolation! During the Winter of 2002–03 it was decided that such a process was too hit and miss, as infection might well come back to haunt us. We therefore got rid of all the plants and removed all the soil in the Paxton House to a good three feet in depth (thanks to Emiliano Sanchez). The houses were then washed down and sterilized, and the rooting area filled with fresh soil. New plants of the same varieties were obtained and have been planted. These are now in the process of being trained into the required condition.

The back wall of the Paxton House carries some shelving, which, together with the floor, provides a home to plants – mostly half-hardy bulbous subjects – which do not conflict with the use of the house as a vinery.

FIGS

A luxury fruit crop that has been grown in the UK for centuries by those with the resources necessary to achieve success, figs were probably introduced during the Roman occupation and have certainly been in continuous cultivation since the Medieval period. The acme of their cultivation was probably achieved during the second half of the nineteenth century when they were cultivated extensively in the glasshouses and walled gardens of the landed and moneyed classes, and were included in the productive garden schedule of any self-respecting head gardener. The production of a crop of figs can still be a reasonably successful enterprise in any home garden if the relatively simple needs and processes of the crop are understood. The fresh fig may be an acquired taste; but once a crop has been produced and ripened on the tree, the flavour and texture will probably make it a 'must have'. It is currently a fashionable fruit (as an imported commodity), and is used regularly in dessert recipes by 'celebrity chefs'.

The fig is a vigorous, extraordinarily tenacious and long-lived tree and, in the process of its cultivation, will put up with what appears to be draconian treatment. If allowed unrestricted growing conditions and a reasonably fertile soil it can develop into a large, bushy tree, up to 15 or 20 ft. in height and spread and, once fully grown, it crops prolifically.

Fruit production in the UK depends on proper 'ripening' of the current season's shoots: the shoot must become mature and woody right to the tip, otherwise frost will quickly destroy the tissues. Although the origins of the fig are obscure, it is most likely to have originated in Mesopotamia. This implies the need for a sunny position and hence, in most parts of the country, training or planting against a south-facing wall. In Cornwall we are fortunate that we can grow and crop figs out-of-doors and without protection relatively easily. The other crucial feature of cultivation is to restrict root growth dramatically so that shoot growth is also restricted and energy is channelled into the setting of fruit buds. This treatment constrains the development of the tree and keeps it within manageable proportions. If the fig is to be planted against a wall it will require about a 15-ft. run and a traditional, sealed brick bed of up to two cubic yards' capacity. This needs to be constructed with a good layer of drainage in the base; but there should be no avenue for the roots to escape out of this constraint and, *de facto*, no drainage outlet. Crop management does mean, therefore, that considerable attention has to be paid to watering in the summer. The fig fruits on the

previous year's wood, having set the fruit by the first Autumn. This fruit-set can be enhanced by stopping the shoots in early Autumn, a process that involves cutting back shoots to the fifth or sixth leaf.

...at... are about the size of a pea ...sat... but survive the Winter ...rem... Winter pruning requires the ...ning of fruiting shoot in ...create a... ng and the thin-...fruit prod... in Summer, to create a... structure for ...We have...

...obtain a ...good range of varieties, selected from those that would hav... ...in the nineteenth century. These were obtained from Reads of N... ...he National Collection of fig varieties. Although we have plant... a wall in the Reserve Garden, the rest have been planted a... wooden half-barrels of four and a half gallons' capacity. These a gravel bed in the walled garden, under the south wall. This per... to be tipped up each year, quite easily, and the roots which have e... pruned back. Now, after three years of judicious pruning, we hav... plants with a suitable framework for fruit production and are begin... the benefits. However, figs are tenacious plants: one on the south-fac... the Walled Garden, probably Brown Turkey, has survived the loss of... house, broken out of its brick box and run wild, yet still produces large... of edible figs every year (see page 113, harvested by John Nelson). It has been persuaded, year by year, to take its proper place on the wall and relinquish its domination of valuable space for growing other crops (above). It was finally constrained to its original place in 2003, but still has a free run for its roots!

VARIETIES

Varieties grown at Heligan are (opposite):

Angelique, a mid-season variety, which needs wall protection. The fruit is medium-sized and roundish, the skin yellow with white dots. The flesh is white tinged with pink, and has a sweet flavour.

Black Ischia, a mid-season variety with hardy, medium-sized fruit shaped like an inverted cone with both ends flattened. It has purplish-black skin and crimson flesh which is sweet and juicy.

Brown Turkey (page 113), an early- to mid-season variety, which is hardy and is the most commonly encountered variety in the UK. The fruit is medium-sized, oval to pear-shaped and ribbed. The reddish-brown skin has a purple tinge, and the deep red flesh is very sweet. The flavour is excellent.

Brunswick, an enormous mid-season variety with large, hand-shaped leaves, which is prolific when well fed. The fruit is hardy, pear-shaped, lop-sided and ribbed, with short stalks and a greenish-yellow skin, tinged brown and with brown dots. The greenish-white flesh, tending to pink, is sweet and has excellent flavour.

Bourjasotte Grise, a fairly large, late-season variety. The fruit is hardy, round or peg-topped with short stems and thin, dark, reddish-blue skin with a strong bloom. The brownish-red flesh, which is yellowish at the base, is jelly-like, with a very rich flavour. This is one of the best figs for flavour.

Castle Kennedy, a very early season, hardy and large variety. Its fruit is long and pear-shaped, with one side always flattened. The light greenish-brown skin has a greenish eye, and the red-stained, whitish flesh is sweet, with a fair flavour.

Negro Largo, a very large, mid-season variety with five-lobed leaves. It is a prolific cropper. The fruit is long, pear-shaped, lop-sided and not ribbed. The skin is thin and deep black with a coppery tinge. The pale, orange-red flesh is crimson at the centre and very rich and sweet.

St Jean, a large, mid-season variety. The fruit is long and pear-shaped, with violet-grey skin and strawberry-red, pulpy flesh with an excellent sweet flavour.

Violette Dauphine, a large, mid-season variety, needing wall protection. The fruit is uniformly pear-shaped; the skin is violet-purple tinged with green, and the pale, strawberry-red flesh has a rich flavour.

White Ischia, a small, mid-season variety with compact habit. It is a prolific cropper. The fruit is peg-topped; the skin greenish-white, tinged red from the flesh, which is deep purple-red, sweet and juicy. The flavour is excellent.

White Marseilles, a large, hardy, early-season variety with five-lobed leaves. It is a prolific cropper. The fruit is round to pear-shaped, slightly ribbed, with a short neck. The skin is pale green to yellowish-white, and the flesh is whitish and transparent, with a rich, very sweet flavour.

CHAPTER 8

SUB-TROPICAL FRUITS
CITRUS FRUITS

Citrus trees were grown on most of the estates of the larger country houses in England during the nineteenth century, as much for the status that the ability to cultivate such an exotic crop inferred as for the yields and quality of the fruit produced. In the very early years of cultivation, from the late seventeenth century onwards, these large trees were housed in purpose-built, heated orangeries – in themselves indicators of wealth, status and ability to be fashionable – usually designed in the classical tradition and having windows on only the front and sides, unlike conventional greenhouses. The orangeries often incorporated complex under-floor heating systems and many highly specialized ventilation features.

The traditional process for growing and managing the trees was to house them over the Winter and then stand them outside for the frost-free period of the year. All the citrus species tend to have highly scented blossoms, and flower during the winter–spring period when the trees are housed, creating a heady scent which permeates the building. The trees often flower at the same time as their fruits are ripening (page 121): the evergreen foliage and the developing and maturing fruit are extremely decorative. Although citrus fruits were grown chiefly for ostentation and the creation of status, they were relatively easy to manage and make into good quality, fruiting specimens, provided that sufficient light and heat could be provided during the winter months and the pests and diseases were controlled.

Our trees, some of which we have now had for six years or so, are grown in the traditional square tubs (on the following pages), with a pair of bent metal hooks incorporated on two opposite sides so that they can be moved in and out of the house on carrying bars, after the fashion of a sedan chair. The tubs are replicas of the wooden containers used during the nineteenth century, and the design was taken from an early photograph of such a tub that was in use here at Heligan (page 120). The citrus trees are housed in the oldest glass structure we have – a heavily constructed, lean-to greenhouse on the south-facing wall of the Walled Garden, probably dating from the early nineteenth century. It was obviously built as a vinery: we found the typical arched foundations

during excavations. The brick floor has been installed during our occupation in order to ease the management of our current cropping programme – citrus in the Winter and pot-grown tomatoes, aubergines and peppers during the Summer. The trees move out on to the terrace in front of the greenhouses for their summer residence. This terrace was constructed for the purpose, as we no longer have the big house with its front terrace on which to stand them and show them off. The range of citrus trees that we grow is not governed by any particular logic other than the need for the varieties to be relatively easy to fruit. Most of our stock came from

The old photograph that inspired the design of our citrus tubs (top); the Citrus House before (middle), and after (bottom) restoration

commercial sources in the UK. Citrus plants tend to be fairly large, and their size determines the size of the container in which they are grown; but they do need to be constrained by judicious pruning. The size of box container most commonly used is about five cubic feet (20 ins. x 20 ins. x 24 ins.). The trees, although growing in any reasonable long-term compost, require considerable attention to nutrient balances to achieve successful growth patterns.

ORANGES

Oranges probably originate from the sub-tropical regions of South-west China and North-east India, and have been in cultivation for three or four millennia in China. As is perhaps the norm with most citrus fruit, the orange is of hybrid origin and not a wild 'species'. Oranges did not appear in cultivation in Europe until around 1450, having taken a considerable time to migrate across the trade routes. Present-day production of the orange is based on a few productive varie-

ties introduced by the Portuguese from the Orient only 300 years or so ago. Oranges are relatively cold-tolerant: some varieties will just about tolerate a marginal frost, and thus lend themselves to container cultivation in the UK with minimal heat input.

Valencia (right) is the world's most important orange. Despite its name, it is not of Spanish origin: the saga of its rise to prominence is bizarre for an orange. It was first noted in the Azores and is probably of Portuguese origin. It was sent from there in the early 1860s to Thomas Rivers, the eminent fruit nurseryman of Sawbridgeworth in Essex, and named **Excelsior**. Rivers recognized its unusual late-fruiting characteristics, and marketed it as pre-eminently suitable for cultivation in orangeries. He sent material to a nurseryman in Long Island, New York, in 1870,

and from there it was supplied to nurserymen in California in 1876 and to Florida in 1877, as **Rivers Late**. In 1887 it was renamed in California as **Valencia Late**, and from there it took off to all the citrus-growing areas of the world and has dominated cropping ever since. It is the most widely grown orange, but nowadays usually as clonal selections with their own names. **Valencia** trees are vigorous, upright and prolific, with medium to large, roundish-oblong fruits. These are juicy, with well-coloured flesh of good flavour and thin, slightly pebbled rind that is easy to peel and has a bright colour.

Navelina, a navel orange originating from California, is chiefly grown commercially in Spain. A small to medium-sized tree cropping in the late Autumn, it produces the earliest of our fruits at Heligan. These are small to medium-sized, round to oval in shape, with smooth rind of a good orange colour. The flesh is juicy and has a good flavour.

Sanguinelli (above and left) is the commercial type of Spanish blood orange. The productive trees are of medium size, vigorous and without thorns. The small to medium-sized, oval fruits have thick, leathery rind, which is extremely smooth, shiny and dotted with red over the whole surface. Maturing in January, the red-pigmented flesh is juicy and sweet.

Seville is the conventional bitter orange, harvested almost exclusively for marmalade production. It is a tall-growing and vigorous tree which is really too much of a handful for container growing except in the tallest of orangeries.

Bouquet de Fleur, a selection of the bitter (or sour) orange, is grown for its highly scented flowers, a few of which are produced nearly all the year round, but mainly during the winter months. It grows as a small to medium-sized, bushy

tree, with curled leaves. It was the variety grown by the Victorians to provide the orange blossom for wedding bouquets, corsages and so on. It is from the flowers of similar varieties that oil of neroli is extracted. Bergamot oil, which should be distinguished from oil of neroli, is extracted from the skin of the fruit of another bitter orange and is used for flavouring Earl Grey tea, among other things. It is possible to obtain some other selections for flower production – the so-called Bouquetiers – but it is difficult to find any in the UK, other than from specialist suppliers.

MANDARIN

The mandarin is originally from China, but the Satsuma mandarins were derived from Japan and are the most cold-tolerant type of orange crop, so lend themselves to cultivation in the UK. **Owari** (page 117 and right) was the commonest commercial satsuma, but is now being replaced by superior selections. The tree is vigorous and crops prolifically, even when young. The fruit is generally a flattened globe, but growing conditions affect the shape. The cropping season is relatively early: the rind of this variety, which separates from the flesh at maturity, does not develop colour fully until after the flesh has matured, so do not delay harvesting. It is virtually seedless.

LEMONS

The lemon is of hybrid origin, but the parentage is obscure and lost in the mists of time. It was probably developed on the Indian sub-continent and was refined in Mesopotamia. Lemons did not arrive in Europe until the Moors brought them to Spain in 1150. Lemon trees (page 124) are vigorous and grow to large sizes, but can be constrained by pruning and thus make good container subjects. The lemon is a valuable decorative tree – not just because of the bright colour of the fruit, but because it tends to produce flowers with a very intense fragrance sporadically throughout the year. This also means that it is possible to have fruit all the year round (from the **Quatre Saisons** types), although the degree of the ever-bearing characteristic varies according to variety. Commercially, the flowering

of the crop is often manipulated to determine the main season of production – a process also possible with container-grown specimens. Lemon trees are often quite thorny.

Eureka is the predominant commercial variety of lemon grown in most parts of the world beyond the Mediterranean region. Of Californian origin, it appeared during the middle of the nineteenth century. It is useful for container production because it is only moderately vigorous, with sparse foliage and a spreading habit that make it straightforward to prune into shape. It also flowers and fruits in an ever-bearing fashion (if not manipulated), and the lemons tend to be produced on the outside of the tree as it is tip-bearing. The fruits, which are of high quality and prolifically produced, are medium-sized, with smooth, yellow skin, thin rind and very acidic juice. They are virtually seedless. The tree has very few thorns.

Meyer was collected in China by F.N. Meyer and introduced to California in 1908. It develops into a small, compact, bushy tree with an ever-bearing habit, so lends itself to container production. It is probably a hybrid between a lemon and a mandarin. The fruits are relatively large, distinctly roundish, but extend into nipples at either end. The rind is very smooth, shiny, bright yellow becoming faintly orange, thin and not aromatic – not good for zesting. Altogether, it is not really a commercial variety, but is good for home growing.

LIME

Bearss is the Californian name for a fruit otherwise known as the **Persian** or **Tahiti lime**, the latter name because it was from Tahiti that it came to California between 1850 and 1880. The origins of this citrus fruit are obscure; but it is probably a hybrid between the acid lime and a citron, and arrived in the West from the Orient having travelled the usual trade routes, via Persia and the Middle East, over several centuries. The lime usually found in retail outlets, it is used extensively in cooking and as an adjunct for flavouring gin and tonic. The tree develops as a smallish, compact bush, and produces small, seedless fruits in mid-winter. These are picked and used green, originally to distinguish them from small lemons! The flowers are uncommonly fragrant. It is not particularly cold-hardy.

CITRON

Citron trees develop as sprawling and untidy, medium-sized trees, which are easily managed by formative pruning and so lend themselves to being grown in containers. They are very susceptible to cold. The fruits (below) are large (six inches long by four inches in diameter), and often irregular in shape; the rind is pale yellow, eventually ripening to orange, smooth but very uneven, thick and difficult to separate from the pulp. It is not a juicy fruit. This particular citrus fruit is used for the commercial production of candied peel: domestically, a slice could be used for flavouring gin and tonic if your habit is to drink out of a bucket! The citron is aromatic in all its parts: the flowers are highly scented, the fruits have a powerful fragrance and can be used to perfume a room, and the crushed leaves were often used as a moth deterrent.

Bhudda's Hand is a peculiar fruit, named because of the way it divides into a group of 'fingers' from the stalk end. The tree itself is small, potentially more of a large shrub.

Etrog is one of the least vigorous varieties, and the chief use of the fruits is in the Jewish Feast of the Tabernacles. The fruit is smaller and yellower than that of the citron, but eventually turns pale orange. More or less lemon-shaped, it is heavily seeded and has an acid juice.

PINEAPPLES AND THE PINEAPPLE PIT

The triumph of successfully cropping pineapples at Heligan without the aid of modern technology was due more to our sheer dogged perseverance in achieving the heating process than to the actual production or cultivation of the plants. Our attempting their cultivation was, quite simply, determined by the fact that a range of what had at first appeared to be deep cold frames was later identified as a traditional, stable manure-heated pineapple pit, which underwent restoration. This provided the impetus to find enough pineapples for propagation to fill this unusual facility, and then to learn how to manage a hotbed warmed by manure.

The Pineapple Pit was excavated by John Nelson in 1991; but at that time its structure and function were a mystery. However, the advice of John Chamberlain, an architect who specializes in old horticultural structures, soon put us right and explained its function and the various layers of sophistication which had accrued over the years. We chose to restore the pit to its 1840–50 layout. This structure consists of a central, deepish (three feet at the back) chamber topped with traditional English frame lights (each six feet by four feet). Both sides of the chamber are flanked by a deep, narrow pit, into which the hotbed material is stacked, once it has been 'fired up'. The brick walls dividing the chamber from the heating pits are hollow, and the base on which the pit is built is a honeycomb structure, so that the heat from the hotbeds can pass into the cavity. The heat then rises to the top part of the internal wall next to the chamber, also built as a honeycomb, so that it can pass into the growing chamber. The pit is oriented east-west, which makes the best use of any available winter light to add heat to the chamber naturally. During the Winter, sailcloth blinds are also run out over the lights at night to provide further insulation and retain heat.

The heating process depended, traditionally, on the hotbed technique. This involves effectively fermenting horse manure at such a pace that the heat released can be used to warm the air in the growing compartments of the frame. This sounds fairly simple to achieve; but, in practice, the process demonstrated many (now obvious) pitfalls and the ignorance created by the lack of the real practical knowledge needed for success.

What is 'horse manure'? The answer seems obvious. We collected 'manure' from many local stables – to fill the heating pits requires 30 tons of the stuff! – and stacked it to start the fermentation process; but it was not a success and never really got going. Despite perseverance, we failed to make much heating for any length of time. So how did our forebears manage? To them, this was such a commonplace activity that they scorned to mention it in their writings. The 'Eureka!' moment came when Tom Petherick, who had spent many years working in racing stables, reminded us that a stable-lad would clear out only the urine-soaked patch of straw bedding and replace it with a similar handful of fresh material.

John Nelson restores new 'pines' to the Pineapple Pit, 1994 (top); a heap of manure (above left) waits to be loaded into the heating trench adjacent to the Melon House (above right)

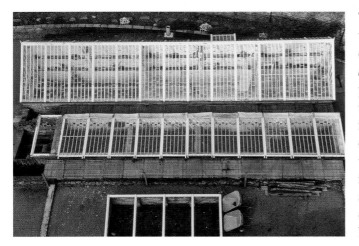

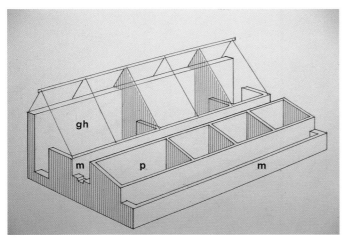

This produced a manure stack with a very high urine (nitrogen) content. Once this *modus operandi* had been established, the problem was simply to obtain the right stuff. This eventually involved recourse to obtaining our supplies from racing stables, which in turn required shipping it in truckloads from considerable distances. It also depended on us finding stables that still bedded horses on straw. However, once we started to stack and manage such material, heating it up was no longer a problem: the trick was to learn how to attenuate heat production so that it did not peak too quickly and at too high a level. After a couple of years this process had been determined, and now manure hotbeds are a piece of cake – we wish!

For successful production of pineapples, the temperature of the chamber in which they are growing should, ideally, not drop below 10°C. Any level above this is a bonus. In fact, a filled pit, suitably managed,

Restored Melon House and Pineapple Pit viewed from above (top); diagram showing (m) manure trenches and (p) pit with Melon House (gh) behind (middle). The Pineapple Pit after initial clearance (bottom) – overgrown Melon House behind

provides heat for just over eight weeks. Once we had cracked the heating process and its control, the constant maintenance of the delivery of such warmth was paramount; but one other part of the learning curve now manifested itself. In our first attempts at using the hotbeds, we duly filled the pits with fermenting manure and stood back. But Murphy had not thought to warn us that both pits would run out of heat at the same time, which they did in due course. The first filling of the pits occurs in the last week of September or the first week in October, depending on the natural warmth of the late season; but if both pits are filled at this time, they suddenly run out of heat, simultaneously, in mid-January. This is potentially catastrophic to the pineapples, should the Winter be at all cold; hence we quickly learnt to fill one pit first and then fill the second some four weeks later, so that when the first pit ran out of heat and

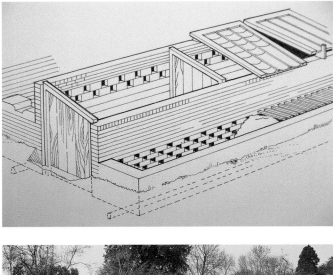

The Pineapple Pit – diagram (top) and reality (above) show honeycomb walls which allow heat from the manure trenches to pass into the pit

had to be refilled the other pit was still warm enough to house the pineapples. This system requires that the back pit is filled three times in a season and the front pit twice: the programme provides sufficient heat to maintain the chamber at a satisfactory temperature over the Winter until mid-April, when the sun becomes an adequate source of heat.

Without an extant pineapple production industry in the UK, finding enough stock (about 200 cuttings) proved a challenge, but the issue resolved itself in a typically Heliganesque way. At that time (1994), a visitor to the gardens engaged us in conversation: he turned out to be a scientist researching pineapple cultivation at the Government Agricultural Research Station at East London in

KwaZulu-Natal, South Africa. He offered to send us material – 100 cuttings each of **Smooth Cayenne** and **Jamaica Queen**, both vintage varieties that were available during the middle of the nineteenth century. These were delivered to the airport at Johannesburg, from where they were transported to Heathrow by KLM (a journey arranged by Tim Smit's father, once a boss man in that airline). We then drove to Heathrow to pick them up, where we had to pay the princely sum of about £14 to clear Customs, the only cost to us from the entire journey. In typical fashion, these cuttings arrived on a bank holiday weekend; so it was all hands to the pumps in order to get them potted up and installed in the propagation case before they dried out completely. Only two or three failed to respond and produce roots, and we managed to pot up the rest in terracotta pots and plunge them into the fermenting tanbark in the Pineapple Pit. Then we discovered our shortcomings in hotbed creation and management. The first Winter caused all the plants to turn blue with cold; but they did not die and by October 1997 we had learnt the process and harvested the first fruit. This was a cause of major celebration, an opportunity to break open the bubbly and invite the television cameras!

Pineapples fruit when they are ready to, after having reached maturity. In any untreated crop, fruiting is an irregular occurrence and can happen at any time of year. Consequently, harvesting and propagation

John Nelson discusses the excavated Pineapple Pit with John Chamberlain (top); Mike Rundle poses for the installation of new pineapple plants (bottom)

'Jamaica Queen' in the Pineapple Pit (above), and
Richard Dee with our first harvest, October 1997 (right)

is a year-long activity and year-round supplies become the norm. Pineapples are propagated from cuttings, which can originate from three distinct regions of the plant. The first type is the 'suckers' that arise from the base of the crown and are known as rattoons. The second region of production is below the fruit on the stalk as the lateral buds elongate and produce a shoot. The last type, that most likely to be available to the amateur, is, of course, the single shoot from the apex of the fruit. It is not prudent to try to cut this out: as the shoot is just enfolding leaf bases and has no central core, each leaf will just peel away. The best way to extract the shoot is to grasp the fruit with one hand and the shoot with the other and twist the latter out of the

top. The shoot is then placed somewhere suitable to cure, in an upside down position: this means drying it out (an airing cupboard is a good place to do this), and after a few days it can be potted up and kept in a propagating case with bottom heat until it is established.

Our young plants are grown in a line inside the front wall of the pit, and when these are potted up they are placed in the middle of the frame, while the large plants that are ready to flower

Pineapple 'Smooth Cayenne' flowering at Heligan (left). John Nelson slices our first pineapple for the team (above)

and fruit are sited, in ten-inch terracotta pots, along the white-painted back wall, where they get maximum light and warmth. Traditionally, the pots were plunged in tanbark, which also fermented to provide heat. Although we were able to do this initially, our local tannery has gone over to using the liquid extract, so we now use active leaf-mould instead.

We now crop pineapples as a matter of course, but the saga of the road to success is pretty typical of the learning curve we have had to pursue for many of our tasks at Heligan.

CHAPTER 9

ANNUALS AND SWEET PEAS

CUT FLOWERS FOR DECORATION

The provision of cut flowers for decorative use in the house was a significant aspect of the Head Gardener's task. It was not only necessary to be able to harvest such material continually from the pleasure grounds, but also to have a programme of cut-flower cropping as part of the production schedules in the productive gardens. Flower arranging, an art in which the Head Gardener was also expected to demonstrate some skill, was usually undertaken by the garden staff. Complex table decorations for dinner parties and other functions, as well as bridal bouquets, corsages and a wide range of both flowering and foliage pot plants were expected to be produced from the garden, largely as a reflection of the sophistication of the proprietor's household. The range and scope of flowers for cutting was extensive and varied, from the formal growing of crops in the productive garden to perennial crops in odd corners and nooks, and it included the use of trees, shrubs and herbaceous plants from the borders of the pleasure grounds.

ANNUAL FLOWERS FOR CUTTING

Annuals were an important part of the cropping schedule in the productive gardens, as the house would have required large quantities of colourful cut flowers for decorative use, not only in the reception rooms but also in the bedrooms. An intensive programme of production was required to grow the vast quantities of annual flowers that were needed throughout the year. These can be broadly divided into those that are hardy, i.e. they can be sown directly out of doors, and those that are not frost-hardy and must therefore be grown under protection in the seedling stage but can be planted out for the Summer – the latter are referred to as half-hardy.

Cosmos 'Sensation mixed' (right)

ANTIRRHINUMS

Snapdragons, *Antirrhinum*, as varieties for cutting, are probably one of the most prolific, colourful and eye-catching flowers that we grow. Their impact is en-hanced by the plants being sited just inside the gate at the top of the Vegetable Garden, next to the central path, so that the visitor is suddenly met with a riot of colour during mid-summer and beyond. Popular as cut flowers until the 1960s, snapdragons, like wallflowers, fell from favour, so suitable varieties that produce a tall, single stem with many evenly spaced individual flowers, making them suitable for cutting, have been difficult to obtain. They are, however, experiencing a minor resurgence, and we can now obtain seed of proper cut-flower varieties again, commercially.

The seeds are sown in trays at the beginning of the year and are placed in a propagating frame at 21°C. Snapdragons grow quite slowly as seedlings, so need the entire Spring to produce plants large enough to transplant to the beds. Germination is slow, but once the seedlings are big enough to handle they are pricked off into cellular trays at the equivalent of 24 plants to a seed tray. These are then kept in a light, warm environment to encourage growth, before being moved, later in the Spring, to a cooler place, in preparation for planting out into the beds when the weather is suitable. The spacing is at a foot square, and they are planted in a six-row bed during the early Summer. The plants establish them-selves quickly and produce their three-foot-tall flower stems from mid-summer onwards. These are in a mixture of colours and produce not only a prolific cut-flower crop but an immediate talking point for the visitor. Once the first crop of flowers has been cut, the plants can be left and a second flush of shorter flower stems is produced for the late Summer. Production entails the growing of some 750 plants for transplanting.

The varieties we grow at Heligan are both F1 hybrids – **Greenhouse cut-flow-er mixed** and **Florists mixed** (left). We also grow a less obviously cut-flower type of snapdragon in one of the lower beds adjacent to the central path. The same production process is followed for this batch of **Picturatum**, a very old strain of *Antirrhinum* developed in the 1840s, which reached the zenith of its popularity at the end of the nineteenth century. The plants are bushier than the cut-flower varieties and produce flower stems up to 18 ins. tall. They have very distinctive flowers of unusual base colourings, which are striped or blotched, principally with white or yellow.

ASTERS

The Victorian 'Chinese Aster', *Callistephus hortensis*, is a good example of a cut-flower and border plant that was popular in the nineteenth century, and which received a great deal of attention in terms of breeding and development at that

time, such that varieties selected then are still available and popular today. These old varieties are mainly in shades of purple, red, pink and white, and are either single (with a central yellow disc) or have various degrees of doubling. The plants are treated as half-hardy annuals and are sown from early March onwards in a seed tray under protection. They are then pricked off into cellular trays at the equivalent of 40 seedlings to a tray. When they have become established they are hardened off and transplanted to the border in the Vegetable Garden, where they succeed the wallflowers. They are spaced at foot square intervals in a six-row bed. A second crop is produced in the same way from a July sowing to replace the Sweet Williams in their border: this crop flowers in the Autumn and lasts until cold or severe weather causes performance to decline. A prolific and generally pest- and disease-free crop, the only likely problem is the incidence of *Botrytis* in the flower heads (especially the doubles) if the Summer is particularly wet. We grow equal-sized blocks of each of the following three varieties for each of the two crops:

Ostrich Plume mixed is the classic, mop-headed double, which grows 15–18 ins. tall.

Sinensis Single mixed (left), from the 1840s, is one of the earliest varieties selected and produces large, single flowers, singly, on stems up to 21 ins. tall.

Giants of California mixed produces single and double flowers. Several flowers are produced on each of the branching flower stems, which grow to 24 or more inches tall.

CLEOME

The spider flower, *Cleome speciosissima* (below), is certainly a plant that arouses curiosity during its long season. The large, unusual corymbs of exotic-looking pink flowers at the top of spiny, three-foot stems always attract much attention and make long-lasting cut flowers. The crop is treated as a half-hardy annual, and is sown in a protected seed tray in March. The seedlings are pricked off into two and three-quarter-inch square or three and a half-inch round pots and grown on to a substantial size in a cold frame until the weather is distinctly clement – usually mid-May. They are planted out at 12 ins. square in a three-row bed that runs right across the cut-flower segment within the Walled Garden, and produce the first flowers within ten weeks of sowing.

MIGNONETTE

Mignonette, *Reseda odorata*, is an ancient cultivated plant with an intense scent that many recognize, but whose origin few can name. The plant eventually grows to a height and spread of nine inches or so and produces very strongly scented, unusual flowers for the duration of the Summer. The unspectacular raceme develops as a conical mass of dirty white with orange flecks, but the saving grace is its phenomenal scent. Although technically a perennial plant, it is treated in the UK as an annual. At Heligan we grow it to line part of the path through the Walled Garden, where it survives for the entire Summer and perfumes the air. Loudon, in his *Encyclopaedia of Gardening* (1822), writes that 'the plant in pots is in universal request, at all seasons of the year, for placing in rooms': it was used to mask the less pleasant smells of contemporary life. We sometimes grow it as a pot plant as well, for decoration in the covered areas. It is possible to grow it during any season of the year with proper attention. The seed is sown in protection, pricked off, hardened and grown on, and then transplanted to whatever situation is required.

HARDY ANNUALS

The seed of this range of annuals can, theoretically, be sown, thinned and grown on *in situ* to produce one crop of cut flowers. However, our ambition is to grow a cut-flower crop from this range of plants over a much longer season: we can, given luck and decent mid-summer weather, extend flower production by dividing the crop into a sequence of three successive sowings. To achieve this long season, we sow the first crop for the earliest flowers indoors in early March and prick off the seedlings into cellular trays, at the equivalent of 40 to a seed tray, as soon as they are big enough to handle. After hardening off, they are transplanted as soon as weather conditions are reasonable. This crop is planted out in the cut-flower section of the Walled Garden on half the allotted space. (In the grand scheme, the cut flower rows are designed to run right across the garden, crossing the path, but this early crop is planted on only one half, as far as the path.) At about the same time as the first crop is transplanted into position, the other half of the rows on the other side of the path is direct-sown into open drills, so that this crop will flower a couple of weeks later than the first. The direct-sown crop needs to be thinned to the appropriate spacing after germination. If the weather of the early Summer has been kind, the first crop is past its best by mid-July and can be removed by the end of that month. It is replaced by a third crop, raised in the same way as the first crop but from a sowing at the beginning of July. This is pricked off into cellular trays and then transplanted to replace the first. These plants flower into October given a modicum of luck and a benign Autumn.

In recent years, June has been a very poor month for light and warmth and our plans have been thwarted, as the first crop has often not peaked until well into July and the second even later.

The range of species and varieties still commercially available is not dissimilar to that which would have been grown a century ago. The pattern for growing is standardized to a double row of each type. For the smaller-growing types, nigella, clarkia and godetia, the spacing is set at 12 ins. between the rows and 21 ins. between the pairs of rows, with eight inches between the plants within the rows. The larger-growing types are laid out at 18 ins. between the rows, with two feet between the pairs of rows and 10–12 ins. between the plants within the rows. The following list gives the names of the varieties we use for cut-flower crops. All are strong-growing and crop heavily and continually in all three phases of the programme:

Shorter-growing types:
Godetia 'Azalaeflora mixed'
Nigella (Love-in-a-Mist) 'Miss Jekyll Light Blue'
Clarkia 'Crown Double mixed' (above, on the right)

Tall-growing types:
Cornflower 'Crown Double Blue'
Cosmos (Cosmea) 'Sensation mixed'
Sweet Scabious 'Crown Tall mixed'
Sweet Sultan 'Crown mixed'

A similar pattern of production is used for the **Larkspur** crop, except that only two crops (both raised from indoor sowings) are used, and only a single row is planted. We grow **Giant Imperial Blue Spire**, which develops tall, upright, single spikes of a purple-blue colour. The plants are grown at 12-ins. intervals in the row. Because of the potentially windy and wet climate, all of the taller-growing types of annuals are supported by stakes and wires.

EVERLASTING FLOWERS

The production of 'everlastings' – plants suitable for the cropping of flowers which are then dried – was also an integral part of the cut-flower programme. In general, the species used were annuals, or were treated as such. The dried flowers were used for winter decorations when fresh flowers were in short supply. The texture of the flowers of these plants tends to be papery at maturity, so they lend themselves to preservation by drying.

HELICHRYSUM

This group of everlasting flowers is of the type that most people have been brought up with and associate with 'dried flowers' generally. They produce almost globular, strong, papery-petalled buds, which flatten to flowers up to three inches across during the late Summer. These come in a range of bright colours, from white through yellow, gold, orange, scarlet and red, to maroon. We grow the traditional and familiar **Helichrysum 'Monstrosum'** (left, with pumpkin) as a mixed-colour batch. Although the seed can be direct-sown and thinned, we tend to sow it in seed trays in the glasshouse and prick off enough plants into modular trays at a density of 24 to a seed tray. These are established in a cold frame to keep the seedlings compact and avoid legginess. They are then planted out into a row in the Vegetable Garden, at nine-inch intervals. Growing to three feet or more

in height, they need to be supported by stakes and wires, but are otherwise little trouble, receiving no attention other than an occasional hoeing. The 30-ins.+ stems are cut as the flowers expand during the Autumn, are lightly bunched and hung upside down to dry in a warm, dry, shaded or dark place, often the Head Gardener's office. Now that we have established a drying shed for our peas, beans and other seeds, the everlasting flower crops are also housed here to dry.

MOLUCELLA

Bells of Ireland, *Molucella laevis*, is another of the old-fashioned, regularly grown everlastings. It is a plant still grown in an unrefined state, there having been no effective selection into varieties. It produces large racemes of green flowers on a lowish-growing, compact and branched plant that can spread to some 2 ft. 6 ins. Towards the end of the season the flowers begin to dry off to brown, a process enhanced by lifting and hanging them up to dry. We raise a few of these plants in pots and plant them out in a row in May.

STATICE

The flowers of this annual sea lavender are produced for drying, ready for use in winter decorations. It is grown in relatively large quantities in the beds in the Walled Garden at Heligan (below), and produces corymbs of small, colourful

flowers in late Summer, born on arching, wiry stems, which extend to about 15 ins. tall. The flowers come in shades of blue, pink, yellow and white, and retain their colours brightly when dried. In order to provide a range of strong colours, we grow **Rosea Superba**, **Market Growers Blue**, **Bonduelli** (yellow) and **Iceberg**, but these old selections are now increasingly difficult to find. The seeds are sown in protection during early April, and pricked out into cellular trays at the equivalent of 24 seedlings to a seed tray. They are planted out in a three-row bed at 15 ins. between the rows and 12-ins. intervals within the row. The plants develop as more or less flat crowns of leaves until the flower stems emerge in July. The flowers are cut in September, when they have developed their full colouring, and are made into small bunches, which are then hung in a suitable place to dry.

OTHER EVERLASTINGS

A number of other everlastings are grown as opportunity crops – i.e. they find a suitable site as one becomes available. Into this category fall **Acrolinium** and **Xeranthemum**, both small and fairly fast-growing annuals. In addition, we grow **Honesty**, *Lunaria biennis*, which is, strictly speaking, a biennial but is treated here as an annual. It is germinated in late Summer and pot-grown for planting out in early Spring in any available corner. It is a crucifer, so beware of the significance to vegetables of club root disease when looking for a place to plant it out.

SWEET PEAS

The history of the development of the sweet pea, *Lathyrus odoratus*, as a cut flower is the usual story of endeavour, chance and the influence of fashion. The origin of the sweet pea as a garden plant dates from the end of the seventeenth century when a Franciscan monk, Fr Cupani, noted a cultivated plant in his monastery garden with flowers half as big again as the wild type. By 1700 he had supplied seeds to a Dr Robert Uvedale at Enfield and also to Commelin, the botanist, in Amsterdam. These first garden plants had deep purple and blue bicolour flowers, and a variety known as **Cupani's Originals** (right, in the Melon Yard) is still available. By 1724 a white variety had been found and lost, and in 1731 Philip Miller had a bicolour white and pink, which eventually found its way to Australia, survived there, and is known as **Painted Lady**. Various new colours and combinations continued to be grown, but it was not until the second half of the nineteenth century that serious breeding work began. Among the many illustrious horticulturists who bred sweet peas at this time, perhaps none is more important than Henry Eckford, who created a string of brilliant new varieties, introduced commercially from about 1880. He was eventually credited with the development of some 115 varieties. Many, known today as **Grandiflora** varieties,

have strong and vibrant colours as well as combinations and stripes, and are characterized not only by their being highly scented, but also by the margin of the standard being flat, as in the species. By 1900, forms with wave-edged standards had emerged in several places. These became known as **Spencer** types, as the first person to note this form was Silas Cole, Head Gardener at Althorp Park, home of the Earl and Countess Spencer. This variant was then pursued and bred throughout the twentieth century with a noticeable loss in scent, due to breeding programmes being concentrated on flower size and colour. However, the final decade of the twentieth century saw a resurgence of interest in the gloriously scented flowers of the grandiflora type, and new varieties began to be created.

Peter Grayson, of Chesterfield, has collected together and maintains an incredible range of 'heirloom' stocks. He sells a very extensive (and inexpensive) range of the seeds of species and varieties – both those he has recovered and those from his own, present-day breeding programme. The list is predominantly concerned with grandiflora types, but also includes early Spencers. It is important to acknowledge his work in recovering, reissuing and advancing these beautiful plants: without his efforts our garden would be the poorer. We grow a few grandiflora varieties each year, not only for the row of cut flowers in the Walled Garden, but also for planting wherever a space is available, so that the scent perfumes the air. Our selection is usually made from the following:

America (1896, Morse) – White striped with red (right)
Black Knight (1898, Eckford) – Maroon and violet bicolour
Captain of the Blues (1891, Eckford) – Deep mauve
Dolly Varden (1898, Morse) – Purple and white bicolour
Dorothy Eckford (1903, Eckford) – White

Flora Norton (1904, Morse) – Clear blue
Henry Eckford (1906, Eckford) – Orange
Janet Scott (1903, Morse) – Pink
King Edward VII (1903, Eckford) – Crimson
Lord Nelson (1899, Eckford) – Navy blue
Mrs Collier (1907, Dobbie) – Cream
Queen Alexandra (1906, Eckford) – Scarlet
Unique (1906, Stark) – White flecked with blue
Violet Queen (1877, Carter) – Violet
Painted Lady (1737) – Rose and white bicolour
Cupani's Originals (1699) – Purple and blue bicolour
(left and previous page)

As we are concerned to have our sweet peas flowering well into the later part of the Summer, when we have large numbers of visitors, we do not begin our crop too early. Traditionally the seeds are sown very early in January, or even before, and are consequently established under protection before being planted out. However, our crop is sown in early February, so does not use up too much valuable space needed to raise other subjects and can be frame-grown more or less as soon as the plants are potted up. The seeds are soaked overnight, sown in cellular trays and placed in the propagating frame. Germination usually takes place within a few days and the seedlings are very quickly potted on into three and a half-inch pots. (Since 2002, we have sown them directly into 'Rootrainers' and planted them out from these.) They are transferred to a cold frame once they have become established, and are allowed to grow on. When the leader shoot has reached about eight leaves it is pinched back to four leaves and the side shoots are allowed to develop. The plants are put out in their final positions after hardening off in late April, at about six-inch intervals, and allowed to grow up the pea-sticks provided. It is very important to cut the flowers regularly if continued flower production and a long season are to be achieved: flower production will diminish dramatically if the blooms are not picked and seed sets. We aim to have our crop lasting until the August bank holiday Monday, when only remnants are still flowering: in the following week the haulms and sticks are rolled up and consigned to the bonfire.

Sweet peas with large flowers and very long stems can be produced by growing the crop as standards. This is done by training a single stem vertically up a cane and removing side shoots and tendrils. An extremely time-consuming exercise, we do not regard it as the most useful deployment of our staff – although we did grow such a crop in our early days, largely to establish our credentials and to prove to ourselves that we could do it!

CHAPTER 10
BIENNIALS

In the general scheme of cut-flower production, there is a limited range of non-bulbous plants that flower during the late-spring to early-summer period. The great majority of these are biennials, or their cropping is managed as if they were biennial – i.e. they are germinated in Summer and established in the first year, then over-wintered to flower and seed in the second year.

WALLFLOWER

The wallflower, *Cheiranthus cheiri* (page 150), sometimes called the gillyflower in older literature, is a well-established bedding plant for the spring border. For these purposes it has been bred intensively to develop compactness of habit, bushiness and intensity of flower colour. However, it was widely grown in the nineteenth century as a cut flower in the productive garden, and was grown as a commercial cut flower until the middle of the twentieth century, virtually dying out as a crop by 1960. For the purposes of cut-flower production, the varieties were selected on the basis of a single, tall flower stem with a long, multi-flowered raceme. Obtaining stock of seed of such varieties proved to be almost impossible until we were able to obtain the entire stock of a variety called **Tall Brown** from a commercial seed firm – they had inherited it in a seed store as part of a commercial take-over! In future it will be down to us to keep the stock going and harvest a crop of seed every four or five years. In 2004 we selected some suitable parent plants from the crop and left these to produce seed. Selection was on the basis of length of the inflorescence and a uniform dark brown-red flower colour.

Our wallflower crop is grown alongside the apple arches on the central pathway through the Vegetable Garden. Wallflowers are cruciferous and therefore susceptible to club root disease. In order to prevent the ingress of this soil-borne disease to our garden we raise all our plants from seed and do not buy in transplants under any circumstances, preferring crop failure if necessary. Wallflowers are biennials, and the seed is sown in the middle of August, thinly, in drills 12 ins. apart, as a catch crop after the onions have been lifted, dried off and removed to the shed to cure. If conditions are dry, the drills are watered in and germination normally occurs in a few days. When the seedlings have produced about nine

leaves they are transplanted to further adjacent rows vacated by the onion crop, at about four inches apart in the rows, which are, again, 12 ins. apart. They are transplanted once more, to the crop site, where they are planted at a foot square, in late October. This transplanting procedure encourages the development of a fibrous root system which allows the plants to make a vigorous start in the Spring. The wet, windy, mild Winters we experience in Cornwall cause an unwanted branching of the stem system to create more bushiness than we would like. This ultimately means more stems and shorter flowers, so we are experimenting with thinning the shoots to get the size of flower that we would wish. Even if the flowers are not up to scratch as a market cut flower, the crop produces useful colour for table decorations in Heligan's tearooms and, of course, the particularly intoxicating scent – the name gillyflower is said to derive from the French *girofle fleur*, literally, 'clove-scented flower'. We are persevering in our efforts to get this crop right.

BROMPTON STOCK

Brompton stock (below, and next page on the left) is a biennial crop which produces flowers with a heady scent in late Spring. It is a member of the family *Cruciferae* and, as such, is closely related to cabbage crops, radish and turnip, as well as being susceptible to the dreaded club root (or finger and toe) disease. Although these stocks could be produced in the same way as wallflowers, it is our practice (because of the generally damp Autumns and smaller number of plants required) to sow the seeds in trays in early September, then prick off the seedlings into three and a half-inch round pots. These are established in a frame and then transplanted to their final positions in late October or early November, after a period of hardening off. They are, however, still grown as an outdoor crop. When these seedlings are planted we tend to drop them into the soil at a greater depth, so that they are braced against the elements. They are spaced at nine inches apart in the row with 15 ins. between the rows. Our crop is grown in the rotated, cut-flower section of the Walled Garden, effectively as a catch crop, and occupies the position used by the cleome crop during the Summer. Because of the usually damp conditions of Winter and early Spring, the quality of the crop is rarely above average; but, again, it is a crop that provides colour and scent for

table decorations when flowers other than bulbs are in short supply. As this crop is susceptible to club root disease, it is important to produce one's own plants and not to be tempted to buy in stock if the crop fails – rather, go without.

SWEET-WILLIAM

Sweet-william (at start of chapter) is an old garden favourite of considerable vintage. Since the beginning of the garden restoration at Heligan, it is one of the cut flowers that we have grown in quantity because it flowers prolifically over several weeks in that 'hungry gap' period of the season. We grow it alongside the central path in the Vegetable Garden (page 149), where it always provides a good show of colour in May and, if the plants are left after the first flush has been cut, it produces a second crop of flowers on the lateral shoots. It is treated as a biennial, sown in the late Summer for flowers early in the following Summer. For our purposes, sweet-williams are sown in late July or early August, in seed trays. They germinate quickly in a convenient space in a greenhouse and are pricked off into three and a half-inch round pots. They are stood in a cold frame to allow them to become established and they grow quickly. As the Autumn arrives they are hardened off, with a view to planting them out in the beds during October or early November, as the weather dictates. They are planted in a five- or six-row bed at a foot square, when soil conditions are suitable and the plants have a reasonable chance of establishment. More often than not, the Winter is wet and the plants look dreadful by the Spring: we debate whether or not to scrap them, but as soon as temperatures increase again they grow quickly and surprise us with their powers of recovery, chiding our lack of faith and rewarding us with a colourful show. They are usually allowed a second flush of flowers as time is available on that site – they are not succeeded until after mid-summer by a late crop of asters. If they grow well in the Autumn, sweet-williams tend to be infected by rust, a fungal disease that causes small, orange-coloured blotches on the leaves during the Autumn and Winter. However, the plants usually grow out of it by the late Spring: if the rust appears to be getting really bad we remove the infected leaves.

CUP-AND-SAUCER CANTERBURY BELL

Campanula calycanthema, the cup-and-saucer Canterbury bell, is a biennial plant which flowers into June. The huge crown of dark green leaves gives rise to a central flower stem, up to three feet tall, the top two-thirds of which carries a long raceme of flowers. The individual flowers are up to, and sometimes more than, three inches long and across, and the trumpet (cup) has a distinct basal corona

(saucer). The original colour was a blue-purple, but the strain that we grow has shades of blue and purple, plus a white and sometimes a pink. The seeds are sown on to a seed tray in early August and germination occurs quickly if they are kept in a warm environment. The seedlings are pricked off into three and a half-inch round pots, and are kept in a cold frame where they become established and grow quickly. They do not like damp conditions and struggle to grow in a damp Autumn, so need to be watered carefully in order to keep them as dry as possible.

The plants grow vigorously and may need to be potted on if conditions are not suitable for planting out. They should be planted out as soon as the site is available – bearing in mind that they do not crop until mid-summer. We grow our crop in the cut-flower segment of the Walled Garden in rows 18 ins. apart, with 15 ins. between plants in the row.

RANUNCULUS

The 'Florists Ranunculus' (on the front cover) was one of the great achievements of floral development in the nineteenth century. It was a plant that received massive attention in its breeding and development and was grown by 'fanciers', much as happened with pansies and auriculas. Ranunculus produces large, usually fully double flowers in strong primary colours, three inches across on 15-ins.-tall stems. They are bought in as corms during the Autumn, having been grown from seed by specialist growers. The corms are usually planted out directly into the ground at this time, but the cool, damp soil conditions of the Cornish Autumn often cause them to rot, so we pot them up in three and a half-inch pots and establish them in a cold frame for a few weeks before planting them out in the ground. Once a good crown of leaves has been developed, the plants are hardened off before the environment of the cold frame causes the leaf stalks to elongate. They are then planted out into the cut-flower segment of the Walled Garden on part of the site to be occupied by the second sowing of the hardy annual cut-flower crops. They are planted at six-inch intervals in double rows 12 ins. apart. The flowers are harvested in May and the crop is quickly cleared to make way for the hardy annuals. We normally grow about 500 corms each year, of the strain referred to as **Peony-flowered** or **Turk's Cap** (page 152).

ANEMONE

Anemones are the earliest of our 'biennial' crops to be harvested and cleared: they have normally finished by Easter. Like ranunculus, the anemones are bought in as corms, and because they are an important cut-flower crop here in the West

Anemones in the Walled Garden (above), and in the Potting Shed (following pages)

Country, it is fairly easy for us to obtain high-grade stock locally. The corms are bought just after mid-summer and, for the earliest crop (Christmas or early New Year), are planted in early July; those for later flowering are set in early August. They are planted in well-cultivated land, a couple of inches deep in drills 12 ins. apart, with about four inches between each corm. It is quite important to plant the corms the right way up – that is, with the claw downwards. They are grown in the rotation of crops occupying the box areas, in the eastern sector of the Walled Garden.

Traditionally the strain grown was **De Caen**. This was superseded by the improved selection, **St Brigid**, but we now grow the still further improved strain called **St Piran**, which has immense flowers. This strain was developed at Rosewarne when it was still a MAFF Experimental Horticultural Station. It had virtually disappeared, but has been resurrected by the Duchy College, now resident at the Rosewarne site, and we are able to obtain stock from this source annually. We grow it because of the Cornish connection.

CHAPTER 11
PERENNIALS

A significant collection of perennial plants is grown both formally and in various niches and corners of the productive gardens in order to provide cut flowers over as long a season as possible.

HERBACEOUS PERENNIALS

The western sector of the Walled Garden is cultivated to provide a series of cut-flower crops. In the principal portion, which undergoes a two-part rotation, one of the segments is devoted to herbaceous perennials that occupy the ground for two seasons. By the end of this time the plants have become overcrowded and require lifting, dividing and replanting in order to maintain productivity. In the course of this process, the site to be occupied moves on in a rotational cycle involving hardy annuals and bulbs. All of these perennials are readily divided. The usual season for propagation is very soon after flowering has finished, as it is at this time that the new season's vegetative growth is beginning.

Aquilegia, the **columbine**, was a favourite cut flower of the Victorians. In the early years it was a plant growing from a crown, with flower stems up to about 30 ins. tall and self-coloured flowers of white, blue, or pink. With the introduction of several species from North America and their use in creating hybrids, the colour range increased: bicolours occurred and the flowers developed a longer spur, hence the **Long-spurred hybrids**.

Coreopsis **Mayfield Giant** (right, in front of the Vinery) is an extremely vigorous and productive plant that flowers prolifically in late Summer. The daisy-like flowers, produced from the vigorous crowns on stems two feet tall, have a slightly humped disc and ray florets of bright yellow.

Doronicum plantagineum **Excelsum**, the first of these cut-flower herbaceous plants to flower, produces large, flat, yellow, daisy-like blooms in April–May, on 15-ins. stems growing from the low crowns. The plants should be propagated immediately after flowering: the crowns divide easily.

Echinacea purpurea, the well-known **cone flower** from the prairie states of the USA, flowers almost continuously for the second half of the Summer. It produces leafy stems with heavy foliage up to five feet tall, and large, daisy-like flowers

with the central cone of yellow-orange subtended by crimson petals (left, with scabious). Cone flowers are readily propagated from seed.

Geum has been part of cut-flower production for 150 years or so. They produce low-growing crowns with branching, wiry flower stems rising to 18 ins. during the middle of the Summer. **Lady Stratheden** has yellow flowers and **Mrs Bradshaw** orange-red flowers.

Limonium platyphyllum (= *L. latifolium*), the native **sea lavender**, was grown principally as a source of flowers for drying. It produces large, billowing, airy heads of tiny flowers in shades of lavender and violet during the second half of the Summer. The leaves are broad, dark green and leathery. It is readily propagated from root cuttings, which are made in the late Winter. We also have some plants of a deep-coloured form, **Violetta**.

Rudbeckia fulgida deamii, the **black-eyed Susan**, is a vigorous and productive herbaceous perennial that flowers from a low-growing crown of spear-shaped, matt green leaves from August onward, for several weeks. The flowers are carried on slender, wiry stems about two feet tall, and are about three inches in diameter, with a brown disc and orange-yellow ray florets. The plant is propagated by division during the late Winter or early Spring: because it is vigorous and prolific, only small pieces are required for regeneration.

Scabious was a common, early- to mid-season cut-flower plant in the kitchen garden. The varieties **Clive Greaves** (blue-flowered) and **Miss Willmott** (white-flowered) were grown extensively, both domestically and commercially, until the 1970s. Scabious is best propagated by division after mid-summer, when it flowers, but the pattern of cropping in the Flower Garden probably means this is delayed until the Autumn.

Tanacetum coccineum, the **pyrethrum**, was a standard in the cut-flower crop of the kitchen garden and, together with scabious, was an important commercial cut flower until the 1970s. There were at least 20 commercial varieties, but these are now quite difficult to find. We currently grow **James Kelway** (which has a yellow disc and red ray florets), **Eileen May Robinson** (deep pink ray florets and a yellow disc) and **Snowball** (white ray florets). Pyrethrums flower during the first part of the Summer and are divided and replanted *in situ* during mid-summer. They do not seem to enjoy particularly the mild, wet climate of the far South-west: our crop suffers losses each Winter, and flower production is sparse compared with the high yields achieved in Eastern counties.

Helenium is a vigorous genus of late but free-flowering perennials, which has seen most of its development as a garden plant since the second quarter of the twentieth century, but a few varieties were developed during the nineteenth century and are still garden-worthy. It has proved difficult to assign the various varieties to particular species: all of the following supposedly belong to

H. autumnale, and all are prolific producers of cut flowers over a long season. *Helenium* **pumilum magnificum** (below left) is an old, shaggy-headed variety that produces deep yellow flowers on two-foot-tall stems from late July into the Autumn. **Riverton Beauty** (brilliant clear yellow flowers) and **Riverton Gem** (reddish flowers, bottom left) appear to date from about the 1880s. They are late-flowering (August into September) and reach four or five feet in height, so need to be supported by posts and wires. They are readily propagated by division or by the individual rooted pieces known as Irishman's cuttings. The three varieties mentioned were obtained from Martin Hughes-Jones of Sampford Shrubs, who holds the National Collection of heleniums.

Our current production of **chrysanthemum** flowers has been limited to the cultivation of a few pom-pom types, propagated annually and grown in rows in the Vegetable Garden. Obtaining period-correct (pre-1905) varieties has not been

easy: it is probable that such varieties could be found, but the time needed to track them down has so far been applied to other subjects. One day we will find material and begin to grow a few of the larger-flowered types in pots, in the traditional manner.

Effectively, the crop is grown as an annual. In the Autumn, when the foliage and spent flowers have been cleared, a few healthy and vigorous crowns are lifted and kept in a frame. In the mild climate of Cornwall, new shoots appear very soon in the New Year and these are taken as cuttings, rooted in the propagation frame, or are slipped off as Irishman's cuttings and potted up. When the shoot has grown to produce eight or so leaves it is pinched back to four leaves to cause it to break. The plants are then

hardened off and planted out when soil and weather conditions permit, spaced at 30 ins. by 18 ins. They grow to 18 ins. tall with at least the same spread, tending to flower from September to November, but varying in this from year to year. They are densely bushy and extremely floriferous, producing ball-like flowers about one inch across. The variety **Bronze Elegance** is old, but we also grow two of its modern sports, **Nantyderry Sunshine** (yellow) and **Purleigh White**. In order to improve the colour range we also grow **Mei Kyo** (lilac-mauve), which is of similar habit and flower, but is an import of the 1940s (all shown above).

Monkshood, *Aconitum napellus*, provides blue cut flowers early in the season. It has the advantage of succeeding in shade and so is left to fill various shady corners, where it produces abundantly flowering clumps which can be left down for several years. The hooded, tubular flowers are produced terminally, in racemes on stems up to about 3 ft. 6 ins. tall.

The genus *Dianthus* has provided many good garden plants. The range of carnation types known as **pinks** has been grown and selected for at least 300 years, and relatively large numbers of old varieties are still available from specialist nurseries. In about the year 2000 we expended much effort on collecting an interesting range of period-correct material, suitable for use as cut flowers.

Many of these are also valuable because of their fragrance. However, the damp, mild climate at Heligan, in both Summer and Winter, proved too much for the majority of these grey-leaved subjects and they rotted off and disappeared very smartly – one of our less successful ventures! But a couple of varieties have proved to be sufficiently resilient and have become established and spread, most notably **Mrs Sinkins** (1868), a highly scented, frilly petalled, fully double, white flower on 12-ins. stems (top left). The peak flowering period is June and July.

The **peony** is an old and well-established plant, both for the herbaceous border and for cut-flower production. It grows annually from a swollen rootstock which carries a series of crown buds. The leaf stalks, often red or purple in colour, develop to about two feet high and carry the divided leaves of rounded leaflets. The flowers, carried on stems about six inches taller, which also have leaflets, are from single to fully double with a series of intermediates. The peony was a much-fancied plant towards the end of the nineteenth century and many varieties of that vintage, from

various breeding programmes, are readily available. The plants benefit from being on a permanent site and are planted at three to four feet apart. The plant dies right back to the rootstock each year. If and when lifted during the Winter, each rootstock can be divided to increase numbers, and growth is reinvigorated by cutting out the less vigorous material. The period-correct varieties we grow in the triangular beds in the Walled Garden are selections of *Paeonia lactiflora*, a late-flowering species and one which has been the subject of intense selection by a variety of breeders. They are: **Baroness Schroeder** (middle left), a double blush flower introduced by Kelway in 1899; **Duchesse de Nemours**, a double white flower introduced by Calot in 1856; **Festiva Maxima**, a double white flower introduced by Miellez in 1851; **General McMahon** (bottom left), a double red flower introduced by Calot in 1867; and perhaps the best known of all peonies, **Sarah Bernhardt**, a double pink flower introduced by Lemoine in 1906.

We have, from time to time, grown some **dahlias** for cut flowers in the late season, but it is extremely difficult to find relevant cultivars – even the National Collection at Ludgvan has only one from 1870.

BULBOUS PERENNIALS

We also grow a significant range of those 'bulbous' plants treated as perennials. These are plants with a specialized storage organ – a rhizome, bulb, or corm, for example.

The **Peruvian lily**, *Alstroemeria* **spp.**, is a South American plant, long cultivated, but which is only nowadays well known. Its current popularity is the result of several modern breeding programmes, which have led to its widespread use as a commercial cut flower. It has progressed from the **Ligtu hybrids** (predominantly orange-flowered) to the **Parigo hybrids**. These come in a broad range of colours, from yellow through orange, to pink, red and white, and on to the variety of colours of the so-called **Princess Lilies** of today's cut-flower market. The Victorians, however, grew at least three of the species for cut-flower production. They are all tuberous and stoloniferous in habit and, once established, maintain an aggressive stance and colonize quite rapidly: they are best left on the same site for several years. The flower stalk carries a terminal group of thin, trumpet-shaped flowers. We grow the following three species, all of which flower in July and August:

A. aurantiaca produces six or seven golden-orange trumpets, up to five inches long, on a three-foot flower stem. The most colourful species, it provided the brilliant orange colours in the Ligtu hybrids.

A. brasiliensis produces four or five narrow, four-inch-long, bronze, red and green trumpets on a flower stem of 18 ins. plus.

A. psittacina produces three or four narrow, four-inch-long, green and red trumpets on a two-foot flower stem.

The latter two species are more interesting than colourful, although well liked by modern flower arrangers.

The exotic-looking, autumn-flowering plant **belladonna lily**, *Amaryllis belladonna* (right), is often found almost semi-naturalized in gardens in the milder parts of Cornwall and the Isles of Scilly. It is a South African plant and, like the nerine, flowers before the emergence of the leaves: the appearance of the large, substantial flowers, as they push out of the bare ground in the early Autumn, is spectacular. The strap-shaped leaves emerge in the Spring and die down by early August, the earliest flowers appearing at the very end of August. They are long-lasting, and the flowering season should go on until the end of October, given reasonable weather. The flower stalk, which is thick and fleshy, grows to about 18 ins. tall, is brownish-maroon in colour, and carries some seven or eight flowers terminally on individual stalks about three inches long. The flowers are broadly trumpet-shaped, about four to five inches long, and variable in colour from a uniform deep pink, to pink and white. These are excellent and long-lasting

cut flowers. The plants are only marginally frost-hardy and require a good deal of sun to develop enough food to enable them to flower consistently and prolifically; hence the usual site for them is under a warm, south-facing wall. Our plants are situated beneath and in front of the arches of the Paxton House. The plant is derived from a bulb, which is left undisturbed for reliable flower production. Eventually the crowded clump of bulbs may push up out of the soil, but to no particular detriment, so long as they are not damaged by frost.

The **Guernsey lily**, *Nerine sarniensis*, is a well-known and long-established flower in the UK, albeit as a pot-grown subject in most of the country. However, here in the mild conditions of the far South-west, several species can be grown successfully outside in a sheltered situation. Nerine is a close relative of the belladonna and succeeds under similar conditions – i.e. in a relatively frost-free position with free-draining soil, adequate moisture during the growing season, and sufficient warmth during the Summer to 'ripen' the bulbs. The species that succeed at Heligan are, like the belladonna, mostly summer-deciduous. Given reasonably stable weather conditions, the flowers last for several weeks and can be used successfully as cut flowers. The bulbs tend to be quite costly, so we have grown them in pots for a few years to bulk them up before planting out. The bulbs are planted out during Summer, just below the surface of the soil with the necks visible, under a south-facing wall, in rows two feet apart with the individual bulbs only a couple of inches apart in the row. They increase reasonably rapidly and are left down for several years, as they tend to flower more freely when crowded together and competing with one another. The following are sufficiently strong and hardy to grow outside under our conditions:

Nerine bowdenii, probably the hardiest of the species and the most robust in our climate, grows out of doors, quite successfully, in favoured situations of Southern coastal gardens. It flourishes in Cornwall and the Isles of Scilly. It has deep pink, umbel-type flowers, which usually emerge in September and are borne on 12–15-ins. stems. This is a winter-deciduous type, the leaves elongating in early Spring and eventually dying back in the later part of the Summer.

Of the commoner summer-deciduous species, *Nerine flexuosa* is the latest to flower: the magenta pink flowers do not appear until November, and the leaves begin to show before the flowers. 'Alba' has glistening pure white flowers. This species has narrower leaves than most, and these tend to be the last to die back in the Summer: in fact, it is very nearly evergreen.

There are many old forms and cultivars of *Nerine sarniensis*, of which **Fothergillii Major** is one of the best known. It produces about ten intense vermilion-coloured florets and emerges in September to early October. The foliage is a distinctive glaucous green. **Fothergillii** has flowers of the same colour as the previous variety, but emerges a week or two later and has green, rather than blue-green, leaves. **Corusca Major** has scarlet-red flowers with up to 15 florets per head. The bulbs are noticeably smaller than those of other varieties.

The Victorians prized the large umbels of the marginally hardy **agapanthus**, *Agapanthus africanus* (right, blue and white). This spectacular South African bulbous plant, with its strap-like leaves and evergreen habit, blossoms for a long period from mid-summer onwards. The umbels of 20 or more gentian-blue flowers are produced on three-foot stems and each floret is about four inches long. There is also a white-flowered form. Agapanthus was usually grown in large pots in glasshouses, but here in Cornwall (in the milder places, at least) it grows and flowers readily outside. On Tresco it has naturalized itself on the sand dunes behind Apple Tree Bay, and it is from here that Mike Nelhams (Curator of Tresco Abbey Garden) collects and dispatches bulbs to us as our border planting increases and we seek to emulate the photographs of the late Tremayne era at Heligan. The plant is grown in the shrub borders and in the south-facing borders in front of the Melon Yard walls, from where blooms are cut as needed.

Crinums are vigorous and exotic-looking South African bulbous plants, and are much hardier than their appearance suggests, provided that they are sited in a relatively warm position and one in which their large, soft, strap-shaped, light green leaves are not able to be damaged by wind. The most commonly encountered form is the hybrid *Crinum × powelli*, which develops substantial clumps with arching, floppy leaves up to 30 ins. tall. The flower stem approaches 36 ins. in height and carries a head of many pale pink, narrow, trumpet-shaped florets, some four inches long, of which only three or four are open at any one time, giving the plant a long flowering season. *Crinum moorei* produces its leaves in a fan arrangement and is a taller, though less substantial and vigorous species: we grow the white-flowered form, **Alba**. These plants are sited in the Walled Garden in an old brick water tank in one of the warmest corners, under the front wall of the Melon Yard, and in various borders under the walls.

The **Indian shot plant**, *Canna indica*, is another half-hardy plant which normally has to be lifted and over-wintered under protection, but which can, in

Cornwall, be left *in situ* all the year round. The exotic-looking plant is usually grown for its foliage in bedding schemes, but, when established, flowers freely and produces long-lasting cut flowers.

Cannas are now available in a wide variety of forms – dwarf or standard, with green, 'purple', or variegated leaves, and flower colours of yellow, orange, rust, pink, salmon and red, with plain, edged and spotted flowers. We have moved our large collection of varieties to the Jungle.

A native of South Africa, the **Kaffir lily**, *Schizostylis coccinea*, lives in damp places such as the borders of streams: like the arum lily, it prefers not to dry out at any time of the year. The value of this plant is its autumn-flowering habit and, under mild conditions, it continues to produce flowers into the early Spring. The plants are rhizomatous and clumps expand quickly under good conditions. The leaves are typically rather like a small gladiolus, 12–15 ins. tall. The cupped, star-like flowers are also set like a gladiolus, on sturdy stems up to about 18 ins. tall. Flower production tends to be prolific in anything like reasonable conditions. As its name implies, the species type is red-flowered. There is also a slightly larger-flowered form, **Major**, and two varieties of old vintage – **Mrs Hegarty**, which is pink and tends to reach its peak flowering period in November, and **Viscountess Byng**, with paler, rose-pink flowers that peak later, usually in about February. They provide splendidly colourful flowers in the depths of Winter.

Although both the large- and small-flowered hybrids of *Gladiolus* are treated as annuals in the Cut-flower Garden (see Chapter 12), the species generally seems to benefit from being left undisturbed for several years in order to establish the corms in clumps, which then flower more prolifically. The following list gives the names of the gladiolus species we grow:

Gladiolus cardinalis, one of the earlier species to arrive in the UK (in 1789), was of tremendous significance in early hybridization schemes. It is a plant from dampish habitats, and in July produces scarlet to red flowers with clean white darts on the lower three petals. It has thick, dark green leaves, from which emerges the arching stem carrying a raceme of five to seven florets.

Gladiolus carneus, which includes *G. blandus* of the early botanists, is one of the many species of gladiolus known as Painted Ladies in the Cape. It can vary from 18 to 30 ins. in height, but usually runs to about 20 ins. tall. The flower spike, produced in June, is lax and often zigzagged, carrying three to ten florets, about two inches across and with a frilly edge to the petals. The colour is usually from mauve to pink, with a blotch at the base of the lower petals.

Gladiolus dalenii is a geographically widespread, variable species that includes the type known to the Victorians as *G. psittacinus*. This limited type from Natal was one of the very earliest – if not the first – species to be introduced to Europe from the Cape, and played an important role in the early development of the large-flowered hybrids. It is a tall plant with the flower spike rising to four feet, and four or five leaves carried in a characteristically flat, fan-shaped pattern. The spike consists of between 12 and 25 florets in an alternate pattern, five or six of which are open at any one time. Although the flower colour in *G. dalenii* covers virtually the whole spectrum of gladiolus colours, *G. psittacinus* was limited to yellows and red, with flaking on the lower petals. It is winter-flowering, and although it grows well after emergence during the Summer, our climate appears to be too rough for the flowers to open: they simply rot off, so we will have to move it indoors in due course.

Gladiolus tristis (left, above) was one of the earliest Cape species introduced to Europe (in 1745), and has been one of the most influential and extensively used in breeding programmes. It is a native of Natal and flowers in May. The plant grows to about 18 ins. tall with the one-sided spike of flowers of three or four florets, each two to three inches long. The colour is yellowish with a dull reddish tinge on the outside. The flowers are markedly fragrant, the leaves fine and rush-like.

Gladiolus undulatus is a species from the South-west of the Cape which flowers in early Summer. The flower stem, usually a single spike, rises to about three feet and carries four to nine florets on a lax stem. The florets are bell-shaped, on a long, tapering, perianth tube; the colour range is white through cream, to pale pink, with deep pink lines on the lower petals.

Tritonia is a genus of small, southern African bulbous plants allied to *Freesia*, *Ixia* and *Sparaxis*. The only species seen at all commonly is **T. crocata**, a plant up to 12 ins. tall, which was much admired by the Victorians as a long-lasting cut flower. It resembles a small gladiolus species, but has brilliant coppery-orange flowers. The corms are small, and care is need during lifting to avoid losing them. The plants are not reliably hardy but grow in our virtually frost-free corners. They are planted in Autumn. The florets are cup-shaped, with rounded petals facing upwards from thin, wiry stems that tend to arch. Several flowers open simultaneously, just before mid-summer. The leaves are narrow and arranged in a fan, like a freesia or gladiolus. There are selected forms, but the only one commercially available is **Prince of Orange** (bottom left) with its intense flower colour. Like many of the species of gladiolus, it flowers more satisfactorily if left undisturbed for a few years, and so is treated as a perennial.

The **arum lily**, *Zantedeschia aethiopica* (above), is a South African plant of sunny, open, but wet grassland, and is able to cope with standing water for long periods. The large, white, goblet-shaped flowers are produced at Easter time in Cornwall. Years ago large quantities of flowers were marketed from crops grown in the marshy, low-lying areas of St Mary's in the Isles of Scilly. In the garden, although they benefit from sun, they are quite capable of producing a good crop of flowers in semi-shady conditions. Our crop is grown in the border under a north-facing wall in the Walled Garden. The soil has been well prepared, with large quantities of well-rotted organic matter incorporated so that the water-holding capacity is adequate. The one point to bear in mind when planting is

that the plants are only marginally frost-hardy and therefore should not be sited in a dip where a frost-pocket is likely to form. Our plants are spaced at about three feet by two feet, and will be allowed to expand considerably before they are moved again (probably a cycle of five years). Traditionally, the golden-yellow spadix was removed from the centre of the flower at picking, so that the yellow pollen did not discolour the pure whiteness of the flower.

The **foxtail lilies**, *Eremurus* **spp.**, from the Himalayas and South-west China, grow from a rootstock which, when lifted, rather resembles a large starfish. The very tall, spectacular stems carry dense spikes of huge numbers of small, starry, trumpet-shaped flowers, with extended golden-yellow anthers, in mid-summer. They are very successful as cut flowers. The rootstocks, which are quite large and fleshy, are available from the usual commercial bulb suppliers. They are dry and brittle when received and should be treated with care: the easiest way to plant them without damage is to take out a trench of sufficient depth for the crowns to be covered by about six inches of soil. They are planted in rows about three feet apart with about 15 ins. between centres, closer in the case of *E. bungeanus*. In June, *E. bungeanus* (= *E. stenophyllus*) produces the smallest flower stem of about five feet tall, with golden-yellow flowers ageing to an orange-brown. *Eremurus himalaicus* produces six-foot-tall flower stems carrying white flowers in July.

Eremurus robustus has pale, silvery-pink flowers, on stems up to ten feet tall, in June. All of these are period-correct for us, although nowadays it is possible to obtain various hybrids with spectacular flowers – the **Shelford hybrids**, for example. We now have a substantial planting of these hybrids in the Jungle, and hope that eventually they can be selectively cropped for cut flowers.

One of the best-known and longest-cultivated garden plants to be grown in this country is the **lily-of-the-valley**, *Convallaria majalis* (left). Its uniquely and strongly scented flowers were prized by Victorians for incorporating in corsages and, as a consequence, the plants were forced and generally manipulated to provide as long a season of flowering as possible. (The forcing of commercial crops was a viable business until the 1960s.) The plant grows from a stoloniferous rhizome and is propagated by

dividing. It grows most satisfactorily in a shady situation: once established, it spreads rapidly and can become invasive, creating a potential problem, but one we are glad to have – see our bed at the bottom of the Vegetable Garden. The plants flower from late Spring for several weeks, and can be forced in the Winter by lifting the dormant roots almost as turfs and growing them in a dark room. This produces blanched growth, which was a highly prized commodity. There is a pink-flowered form, *rosea*, but we have never grown it.

Dierama (Sparaxis) pulcherimum is the **South African wandflower**. It develops a substantial crown of tall, stiff, narrow leaves from a swollen, fibrous rootstock, from which the inflorescence is produced in late Summer. The flower stalks are long and graceful, like fine fly-fishing rods, up to six feet tall. The individual bell-shaped florets droop from these slender stems and are shades of pink, purple, white and mauve. *Dierama dracomontanum* is an altogether smaller version, with flower stems up to about three feet tall.

We grow a number of **watsonias** of various flower colours, but mostly they are the **Tresco hybrids**: we have not yet made a proper effort to source particular species. Watsonias are first cousins of the gladioli and resemble them in size and shape; but they are in general less hardy, and only suitable for outdoor cultivation in the far South-west and on the Isles of Scilly. They grow from a corm and flower in late Summer – the plants we grow are about the same size and height as the large-flowered gladioli, and come in shades of pink, peach and orange. They make excellent cut flowers.

Pancratium maritimum is from Southern Europe, especially the Mediterranean coast. It grows from a very large bulb, producing two ranks of strap-shaped leaves, from the centre of which the one-foot flower stem emerges in late Summer. This stem carries a loose umbel of highly scented, vaguely daffodil-like, white flowers. The plant is winter-deciduous and should be left undisturbed so the bulbs crowd themselves, as this seems to produce a more prolific flowering.

WOODY PLANTS FOR CUT FLOWERS

In various places in the Walled Garden we have used any available wall space to train a number of woody plants with a view to using them for cut flowers. The impact is also decorative, especially so with those trained as espaliers or fans.

Camellia reticulata **Captain Rawes**, an important camellia variety, was the first of this species to be introduced to the West. It is known to have been grown at Heligan from very soon after its commercial introduction until the 1960s. Three plants are being established and fan-trained on the north-facing wall in the Walled Garden. The large (four inches plus in diameter) semi-double flowers are a bright coral-pink, and are produced in the Spring.

Magnolia grandiflora **Exmouth** (left) is a summer-flowering, evergreen magnolia, a specimen of which survives by the wall in the Sundial Garden, where it had clearly been espaliered. More recently, four trees have been established on the north-facing wall in the Walled Garden: they too are being espaliered. This variety was chosen because it would have been the only variety available during the nineteenth century, largely due to the fact that few selections were propagated and Exmouth is the local clone. Flower production is precocious and tends to be sporadic right through the Summer and into Autumn. The flowers are very large and are highly scented.

The **wintersweet**, *Chimonanthus praecox*, is being trained on the east-facing wall of the Walled Garden to provide its strong-scented flowers for use in Winter.

The **Moroccan pineapple broom**, *Cytisus battandierii*, is a tall, sparse shrub that lends itself to training on a wall. The grey, silkily felted, laburnum-like leaves are decorative, and the cone-shaped clusters of bright yellow, broom-type flowers are pineapple-scented, appearing just after mid-summer.

CUT FOLIAGE

Although most of the cut foliage we use is gathered from plants growing in the pleasure grounds, those subjects required regularly and in reasonable quantities are grown and harvested as crops in various parts of the kitchen garden. Most of the plants we use for this purpose are evergreen.

The single largest requirement is for the lightweight, light-green-leafed stems of *Pittosporum tenuifolium*. The large quantity needed is provided by a block of shrubs filling in the corner of the top jib piece in the Vegetable Garden. They are planted relatively closely (at five feet by three feet), and the regular pruning that occurs with the harvesting of the crop constrains their height and spread.

Once established, the plants develop into low-crowned pollards, which produce strong upright annual growth up to six feet in height. Heavy, broad, dark green foliage is collected from a short row of *Camellia japonica* **Donckelaerii** in the south border of the Walled Garden. As with the pittosporum, once the crown has been developed and the material is cut back annually, strong straight shoots are produced. An intermediate type of foliage is provided by *Myrtus communis*. Its foliage is particularly useful for bouquet work and was usually included in wedding garlands. The small, white, powder-puff flowers are interesting and were used as cut material. There is also a short row of *Luma apiculata*, a close relative of the myrtle, but with a more upright habit, a decorative red bark, broader leaves and creamy flowers.

Olearia macrodonta (below with *Callistemmon*, both in flower) is a New Zealand shrub widely cultivated in Cornwall. Uninhibited, it grows to ten or 12 feet high, but is easily constrained to three or four feet by pruning for foliage. The leaves are thick and leathery, holly-shaped and grey-blue in colour. The marginally hardy Australian shrub *Callistemmon citrinus* is also kept within bounds by pruning the foliage, but is unlikely to flower with this treatment. The leaves are green, leathery and willow-like. We also grow a range of native ferns in various shady corners of the garden to provide a variety of foliage in all but deepest Winter.

CHAPTER 12

BULBOUS PLANTS

This group of plants includes all the bulbous cut-flower crops that are grown at Heligan and are (usually) lifted annually, and which fit conveniently into various niches of the overall rotational cropping scheme. Bulbous plants that are left *in situ* for more than one year are dealt with in Chapter 11, which is devoted to perennials. The group 'bulbous plants' includes not only plants with bulbs but also those with corms, tubers and other similar annual storage structures. In order to ease the actual practice of cultivation, most of these crops are planted in rows spaced 18 ins. apart – this also simplifies planning the layout on the ground and management generally. The intensity of cropping is thus governed by the particular spacing within the row, which depends primarily on the bulb size, but also on the size of the plant above ground.

IRIS

The production of cut flowers in the early Summer has for long been dependent on the great diversity of plants from the genus *Iris*. It is a huge genus that has spread throughout the Northern Hemisphere in both the New and Old Worlds, and has very closely related genera in the Southern Hemisphere. Irises in the Victorian cut-flower garden would have been largely from those groups loosely defined as 'bulbous'.

The earliest to flower is *Iris tuberosa* (which has since been transferred into its own genus as *Hermodactylus tuberosus*). In Cornwall it is usually in flower by early April, after an autumn planting. The thin, very erect, wiry stems rise to about 12 ins. tall and carry the reed-like, four-sided leaves. The flower is, however, the startling feature: often described as 'peculiar', it is some two inches across and sombre-coloured, with dark purplish-black spotted falls and bright yellowish-green standards. This variety was commonly known as the **snake's head** or **widow iris**. It is a vigorous plant, despite its delicate appearance, and multiplies exceedingly well if given reasonable treatment. It can be forced, and grows from a small, elongated, worm-like tuber.

The **mourning iris**, *Iris susiana*, is one of the few easily grown members of the **Oncocyclus section** of the genus, and originates from Turkey and Iran.

Rows of English iris in the Walled Garden

It has been in cultivation since 1572 and was much valued by the Victorians, but is nowadays as rare in the trade as it has ever been: we are currently unable to obtain it. It grows from a rhizome and is best planted in late Autumn, as the scythe-shaped leaves appear early (before Christmas) and it flowers in May. The flowers are carried on stems usually 12–15 ins. tall; they are relatively large, broad and substantial, with a creamy-white ground, purplish veining, and a purple blotch on the falls.

The **Spanish iris** is derived form *Iris xiphium* and, as its vernacular name implies, is a native of Iberia. It grows from a squat, largish, netted bulb, which, if planted in the Autumn, flowers by early June. It is most satisfactorily treated by lifting the bulbs in the late Summer, drying them off, and then replanting them four inches apart in the row. This achieves good productivity: the flowers tend to decline if the plant is left unattended. The flowers are produced on stems about 20 ins. tall and come in shades of blue, purple, yellow and white. Not long ago it was still possible to obtain named selections, but nowadays only mixed selections can be found – and even then, not always. Its popularity has been overtaken in the commercial cut-flower market by both the productivity of the Dutch iris and the fact that this packs and travels better.

Iris bucharica *flowering in the Vegetable Garden, with rhubarb and forcing pots*

The **English iris** (page 177), derived form another Iberian species, *Iris xiphio-ides*, has suffered a similar fate at the hands of the Dutch iris. However, the English variety has a number of advantages for the home cut-flower grower in that it flowers later (well into July), and the flowers are more substantial and can be very deeply coloured. It is a vigorous plant, developing from a large, tall, netted bulb that produces stems up to two feet tall, carrying the large, flat flowers in shades of blue, mauve, purple and white. The variety **Mont Blanc**, with white flowers, was listed until recently, but other named varieties seem to be unobtainable, although we do have some stock of a new local selection named **Duchy Blue**. It is time that the fortunes of this group of irises were resurrected: the plants are excellent for the home producer wanting late-flowering iris. English iris should be planted four inches apart in the row.

The star of our iris collection is *Iris bucharica*, one of the few **Juno section** irises that is readily and successfully grown in a kitchen-garden setting. Flowering early and prolifically, in March, it is a bulbous iris that produces characteristically broad, pale green leaves up the 15-ins. stem. The flowers, which are produced five or six to a stem, are about two inches tall by two and a half inches wide. They are basically creamy white in colour, with a very conspicuous deep yellow blade

to the fall. The standards are rudimentary and give the flowers a somewhat flat appearance. Under our conditions, this plant multiplies the number of its bulbs of flowering size by three each year and is thus hugely prolific. It is planted in the Autumn, and fairly close together – four bulb clusters to a foot run of row.

CAMASSIA

The camassias are a small genus of plant from Central America that vary in size, but all produce true bulbs. They are, in general terms, both prolific in flower production and productive in bulb multiplication. They require a good level of soil fertility and a relatively sunny and warm climate to succeed best, but the bulbs will survive winter frost if the soil surface is lightly mulched. The bulbs are planted in the late Autumn and are lifted and stored over the late Summer. The flowers are long-lasting when cut.

The most spectacular is *Camassia leichtlinii*, which develops an erect flower stem up to at least 30 ins. tall, terminating in a long, upright raceme of flowers in early May (below). The leaves are stiff and erect. **Alba** has white flowers, while those of **Caerulea** are an intense deep blue. The bulbs are spaced at six inches apart in the row.

The **Mexican quamash** (once known as *Camassia esculenta* but now *C. quamash*) is a smaller plant with a 12–15-ins. flower stem, and a truncated flower in a slightly lighter shade of blue. The bulb is edible and was/is a food plant of the Native Americans in parts of Central America. This plant is very generous in bulb multiplication. The bulbs are spaced at four inches apart in the row, and flower production is extremely prolific.

BRODIAEA

The name 'Brodiaea' is among the most confusing of generic names applied to North American bulbous plants, chiefly because it seems, over the years, to have been a taxonomist's dream. The variation within the genus has allowed taxonomists to create or re-use various other names, such as *Dichelostemma*, *Triteleia* and *Ipheion*, and then to shunt various species here and there among them. However, the most likely synonym to be used in current catalogues is **Triteleia**. The plants described here are Californian and resemble a small agapanthus, both in shape and colour. These species flower during and after mid-summer, and provide a useful bulbous cut flower between the Spring and autumn seasons: the flowers are long-lasting when cut. The bulbs are planted in the Autumn, and spaced at four to six inches apart, as the flower heads are quite large.

Brodiaea laxa (right, middle) is a vigorous and prolific plant that produces a significant annual increase in bulbs as well as a reliable crop of flowers. The flowers are produced in an umbel on a stem about two feet tall, the individual florets being tubular in shape with a slightly flared mouth. These are about two inches long. The flower colour varies within the species, through blues and purple, but the commercially available stock has deep violet-blue flowers. A plant listed as **B. corrina** (right, top) is very similar but slightly less vigorous, and has slightly smaller and more refined inflorescences. It flowers at the same time as *B. laxa* and has more or less the same coloured flowers.

ORNITHOGALUM

One of the longest-lasting cut flowers is the South African **chincherinchee**, *Ornithogalum thyrsoides* (right, bottom). This relative of the better-known Star of Bethlehem was readily available in the nineteenth century, and eventually became a popular commercial cut flower for 30 years or so after the Second World War – it is still occasionally seen, in season, in florists' shops. The genus is a large one, and consists of a hundred or so species, which range from

Southern Europe and Asia Minor to Southern Africa in origin. The chincherinchee produces a very tight and compact raceme, about four inches long, on a stem about 12 ins. tall. The florets are star-shaped with white petals and prominent yellow stamens. The plant is not hardy and is generally planted in the Spring, to flower in late Summer. After the leaves have died down, it is lifted and stored over the Winter as a dry bulb. The bulbs are fairly substantial and are planted six inches apart in the row.

IXIA

This genus of elegant, graceful and colourful cormous plants is native to Southern Africa, and is similar to the gladiolus, to which it is closely related. The genus

consists of about 30 species, many of them reasonably readily available during the Victorian era. Obtaining them today is less easy, but it is still possible to buy some from conventional commercial sources. The trade is now predominantly in the extensive range of hybrids, in virtually the entire colour spectrum. These have been developed in the intervening years, chiefly for cut-flower production, both as mixed seedlings and named varieties.

The various species of ixia were among the very first bulbous plants to be comprehensively collected and sent to Europe from the Cape. They have declined in popularity since about 1970, largely because of their suspect hardiness, but they deserve a better fate than to be consigned to oblivion! The species and early hybrids were grown extensively by the Victorians for cut flowers, usually in pots protected over the Winter to save the emerging leaves from frost in all but the most favoured areas of South and South-west England. Nearly all the species and hybrids readily available should be planted in the late Autumn, or, if the climate is suitable, in the early New Year period. Such late planting seems, by the later emergence of the leaves, to reduce the incidence of leaf disease dramatically. The temptation to plant any earlier (in September, for instance) should be resisted, as the leaves will appear in November and then be subject to all the adverse conditions. All of the ixias, whether species or hybrids, are usually grown from corms, and these multiply readily by offsets. Propagation from seed is easily achieved, but the offspring are likely to be of hybrid origin and hence very variable. Only the species, when grown in isolation, will breed true. The corms, although relatively small (less than an inch in diameter), are of typical corm structure and shape, being somewhat conical and producing offsets abundantly and regularly. They are spaced at a maximum of two inches apart in the row. The upright, narrow, linear, sword-shaped leaves appear during early Spring, the flower spike developing in late Spring to early Summer. After this the leaves continue to grow into the Summer, eventually dying down and drying off in late Summer. The colourful and handsome, wide-mouthed or star-shaped flowers are produced in a raceme on stiff, upright, slender, wiry and remarkably strong stems that reach a height of 15 to 24 ins. Generally there are ten to 12 flowers on each stem.

Of the species, the most desirable is probably *Ixia viridiflora*, brought to Europe in 1780. It has flowers of an extremely unusual shade of electric blue, and is much sought-after by flower arrangers. However, it is rather temperamental. Some of the oldest hybrids have survived in the Isles of Scilly, where they were cultivated as a market cut flower until the 1950s. The commonest of these to be found today is **Early Surprise** (page 182, bottom right, which is not dissimilar to the old Nelsonii): the 18-ins.-tall stems carry about ten flowers, each cerise petal of which has a white stripe down the middle. As the name implies, it is an early-season variety. **Smiling Mary** is also enjoying something of a renaissance. It is

a mid-season variety, and has deep pink and white flowers with purple eyes. **Mozart** is a yellow-flowered, mid-season variety which is also still being grown in the Isles of Scilly. Other named hybrids can be obtained from the trade: we have **Rose Emperor** (page 182, top right, pink), **Castor** (violet-purple flowers with darker centres), **Hogarth** (page 182, top left, creamy yellow flowers with purple centres), which is the latest to flower, and **Vulcan** (page 182, bottom left, dark carmine-coloured flowers).

GLADIOLUS

This genus contains as many as 200 species with a widespread distribution through Southern Europe, Asia Minor and the Levant, across into Central Asia, and then in Africa from the coastal strip in the North, southwards across the continent to the Cape. It is from Southern Africa that the most colourful species and the greatest range of diversity originate. The earliest introductions of these Cape species into Europe – and more especially Great Britain – had occurred by the middle of the eighteenth century, and by the end of that century a considerable range was available. Inevitably, many of the horticulturists of that period began to hybridize the plants, and several lines of development were begun. Many of the species in the British climate flourish if left undisturbed for several years, and are best treated as perennials (see Chapter 11). However, most of the hybrids are best dealt with annually and so are lifted and replanted each year. Also cultivated on an annual cycle are the European species such as *G. byzantinus*, but we do not grow this currently as cormlet production is sufficiently prolific to enable it to become an invasive weed. All of the varieties listed here are planted in the late Autumn or early Spring, and are spaced at three or four inches apart in the row. The plant known as *Acidanthera bicolor*, now *Gladiolus callianthus*, is from the uplands of Ethiopia and thus only marginally hardy, so it is also cultivated on an annual basis. It is a very useful late-summer cut flower, producing its racemes on an arched flower spike some 2 ft. 6 ins.–3 ft. tall, and carrying about six florets. The nodding florets have a long perianth tube and a star-shaped mouth; the petals are white with a deep purple blotch at the base of the upper segment. The variety **Murelae** (opposite, top left), a vigorous plant that increases prolifically, is a Dutch selection and is usually the only form available. It is planted in the Spring and has to be lifted quite late in the season. Also in this category of late-flowering, spring-planted species is *G. purpureo-aureatus*, now sunk in *G. papilio* (opposite, bottom right). It was the species used by Lemoine to introduce mauve into the breeding programme of large-flowered hybrids, and is characterized by the purple and yellow colouring of the nodding, hooded florets, which are produced in racemes on a three-foot stem.

Rows of Gladiolus *Robinetta and Nymph*

The large-flowered hybrids are the best-known line of development today, but initially the hybrids of smaller stature were just as popular. So far, we have been unable to source a contemporary large-flowered hybrid – indeed it would be interesting to know if any still exist: any of the hybrids from the *G. gandavensis* group and *G. Brenchleyensis* would be a notable find for us. The earliest groups of hybrids to become commercially available were all dwarf (up to 30 ins. tall). The first was the *G. × colvillei* group that appeared in 1823, and resulted from crosses between *G. cardinalis* and *G. tristis* made by James Colville, a nurseryman of Chelsea. These plants were principally a race of orange- and red-flowered plants and were quickly superseded; but still surviving from that tranche is **Albus** (1826), which has white flowers with pink anthers. Subsequently the same cross was made again and produced **The Bride** (1871, previous page, top right), which has white flowers with white anthers.

Later in the nineteenth century, *G. cardinalis* was crossed with *G. blandus* (now included in *G. carneus*) in Holland, to produce what became known as the **'Charm' hybrids**, *G. × ramosus*: some of these and their successors are still grown today. We have **Charm** (previous page, bottom left), which has deep rosy pink flowers, and **Robinetta** (previous page, middle left), which has deep red flowers with a creamy edge. Later, these were back-crossed with *G. cardinalis* by several breeders, to give rise to a group which became known as the **'Nanus' hybrids**, *G. × nanus*. Many of these varieties are still widely available today, although several have disappeared during the last decade or so. The hybridization of this group continues, and new introductions appear regularly. Although most of the available named varieties of the Nanus group are relatively modern, several older cultivars can still be obtained. Of these **Elvira**, which has very pale pink flowers with red blotches, is mentioned by Robinson in the 1900 edition of *The English Flower Garden*, and is still easily obtained. **Nymph**, which has whitish-pink flowers with deep crimson flaking, is said, in the 1995 van Tubergen catalogue,

to have been introduced by Thomas Hoog 'more than eighty years ago', and is also readily available. **Guernsey Glory** is more recent and has bright orange-red flowers. Of the vintage varieties, **Ackermannii**, **Blushing Bride** and **Peach Blossom** were all offered in catalogues until about 1990, but, since then, seem to have disappeared completely. Four years ago we did have **Ne Plus Ultra** (page 185, middle right), but lost it in a season when rust disease was particularly rife.

Species gladioli grown at Heligan as perennials are described in Chapter 11.

SPARAXIS

This genus is limited to a small number of species of South African bulbous plants that are closely related to both *Ixia* and *Freesia*. The species that we grow, *Sparaxis tricolor*, is the well-known and colourful type which produces its flowers in mid-summer on wiry, ten-inch stems, with several florets up to two inches across on each stem, all opening at the same time. It was introduced to Europe as long ago as 1780. There is a wide range of flower colours: this species is chiefly orange with a yellow throat, but has pink through to purple flowers. Much stock sold today is of hybrid origin and involves *Sparaxis grandiflora* and *Streptanthera cuprea*. The flowers have a yet wider range of colours and a deeper-coloured throat. The leaves are short and arching in a narrow fan, up to about six inches tall, and the flower is a flared, erect trumpet. The crop is grown in conjunction with ixia, ixiolirion, brodiaea, etc, all of them having similar small corms flowering at much the same time and receiving the same treatment. The corms are spaced at about two inches in the row. They flower in early Summer, but are only suitable for outdoor culture in areas with mild Winters.

IXIOLIRION

This small genus of bulbous plants of the lily family occurs from Turkey across to Afghanistan. Usually only *Ixiolirion montanum* (now *I. tartaricum*) **var. pallasii**, from the area around the Caspian Sea, is obtainable commercially. The flowers are loose umbels of lavender-purple with narrow, trumpet-like florets, about two inches across. Superficially, they resemble a smaller *Brodiaea*. The florets are carried on stems to about 15 ins. tall, and the flowering season of this form is fairly late – approaching mid-summer – so that it usefully fills the gap when the great majority of spring-flowering bulbs are over. It flowers readily and reliably, makes a good cut flower, and has the added advantage of being cheap. Planting takes place in the Autumn, and the narrow, strap-like leaves appear in early Spring. These can be damaged by spring frosts, so the plant is suitable for growing outside only in mild areas.

LEUCOCORYNE

This very small genus from Chile is allied to *Brodiaea* and is represented in cultivation by only two species, of which only ***Leucocoryne ixioides*** is obtainable – rarely, at that. The other is ***L. purpurea***, although the names seem to be used fairly indiscriminately. The species are not hardy, and are therefore only suitable for outdoor culture in areas with mild Winters. They have narrow, thin leaves, and the flower consists of a loose umbel of six to eight florets on a stem about 15 ins. tall. The florets are tubular, about one and a half inches long, and have spreading, flared perianth segments. In Cornwall the flowers are produced out of doors during late April and May, from an autumn planting.

LILIUM

Lilies form a huge and varied genus with a wide distribution, chiefly in the Northern Hemisphere in both the New and Old Worlds. The species have been much hybridized and the number and variants of these is now legion. The few plants described here are the species, forms and few elementary hybrids that were readily available in the nineteenth and early twentieth centuries and were commonly used for cut-flower production. The huge multiplicity of varieties available today is a twentieth-century phenomenon, the result of hybridization programmes. Most of the lilies described here need to be planted with at least three or four inches of soil above the bulb, if only to provide a brace for the tall stems. Although the soils of their native habitats may be very different, virtually all of the various species described succeed in well-drained kitchen-garden soil. Traditionally, lily bulbs are planted in the early Spring and most flower in the second half of the year. The only criterion affecting the productivity of individual plants may be the degree to which the soil is open to the sun: some species prefer cool soil conditions.

The incomparable **golden-rayed lily**, *Lilium auratum*, from Japan is one of the most spectacular, beautiful and heavily scented of all the species of the genus. Unfortunately it is now extremely difficult to obtain and those bulbs which do appear, especially those imported from Japan, are often infected with viruses. It is not many decades ago that this magnificent plant could be reasonably readily purchased, even if it was somewhat expensive. The stem can grow to eight feet in height and carry as many as 20 horizontally presented florets which are each about eight inches across. These are a broad, flat funnel in shape, and the segments are thick, stiff and waxy. The colour is basically white, but superimposed with a central yellow band to each segment and various yellow and crimson spots over the whole surface. The form ***L. auratum platyphyllum***, with somewhat broader leaves, is obtainable slightly more easily and is just as spectacular.

The flowers are, if anything, larger, albeit slightly less marked. The bulbs are also large and should be planted deeply, with at least six inches of soil above them, as they are also stem-rooting. The variety **Virginale** has white flowers, but is otherwise similar to the type. We have now obtained from Japan, through the good offices of Martin Davis of Gloucester, a few bulbs of material raised from seed of *Lilium auratum* itself – the **ssp.** *latifolium*, the **var.** *rubrovittatum* and **var.** *platyphyllum*.

The **Madonna lily**, *L. candidum*, is a European species that has been in cultivation since time immemorial. It develops a stem up to about four feet in height, and this carries the numerous, pure white, funnel-shaped flowers. The colour was associated with the Virgin Mary during the Middle Ages, hence the plant's vernacular name. It does not take kindly to regular upheaval, so we tend to keep it in a semi-permanent bed with the peonies and pinks, where we can also increase the lime content of the soil, which it prefers.

Lilium martagon is another species with wide distribution across the warmer temperate regions of Europe (including the UK) and Asia, from Iberia right across Central Asia towards China, and is therefore variable in its characteristics. It is usually a plant of the lightly wooded slopes of mountains, often seen in glades and sometimes in grassland. In cultivation it can grow to about four feet in height, bearing many of its pendulous, waxy, Turk's-cap-type florets after mid-summer. The flower colour can be quite variable, but in commercial stock is normally a purplish-pink with dark spotting. There is a white-flowered form called **Album**. It succeeds reasonably well in the cut-flower bed, as long as it is not in full sun, but tends to lose vigour when moved every year.

Lilium hansonii (right), from Korea, has been in cultivation since at least the third quarter of the nineteenth century. It is an impressive, martagon-type lily, flowering just after mid-summer, with yellow, orange-peel flowers. The stem grows to about five feet and carries about ten flowers, each up to three inches across. The segments reflex and are spotted with brown. It is a plant that benefits from the sun, but which succeeds best if the bulbs are shaded. A prolific plant, it succeeds well in good kitchen-garden soil.

One of the easiest lilies to grow is the Chinese *Lilium henryi* (next page, middle), introduced to cultivation in the last quarter of the nineteenth century. It is a very tall lily with stems reaching up

to eight feet in height and carrying a very large number of flowers – usually in excess of 20. It therefore needs support, especially if good quality, straight, cut-flower stems are required. It often has two florets on the horizontal flower stalk. The florets are of the martagon type and are usually deep orange, occasionally deep yellow, in colour with light brown spotting. It flowers late, continuing into late August, and is a robust grower in well-drained, strong, kitchen-garden soil. The bulbs need to be planted with at least six inches of soil covering them, due to the eventual height of the plant.

The **tiger-lily**, *L. tigrinum*, now *L. lancifolium*, is probably one of the best-known, most easily grown of the lilies. It particularly lends itself to cut-flower production as it flourishes in a kitchen-garden soil. It is most commonly offered as the type **Splendens**. This plant develops a stem about four feet tall and carries up to 20 or so bright orange-red, Turk's-cap-type florets, with numerous dark spots to the base of the tube. It is characterized by the production of bulblets in the axils of the leaves. A yellow-flowered form is also commonly available.

The **regal lily**, *L. regale* (bottom left), is another of those lilies that are extremely easy to grow, are productive, and make excellent cut flowers. It is a Chinese species and was introduced by E.H. Wilson at the end of the nineteenth century. The stems grow up to about four feet tall and carry many fragrant, trumpet-shaped flowers, each about five inches long, in July. The segments are shining white with a yellow throat inside, and are stained with rose and mahogany towards the base on the outside. The ends of the segments begin to recurve,

giving the mouth a considerable width. This is a stem-rooting species and so should be planted reasonably deeply. A white-flowered variety, **Album** (top right), is also available.

The Japanese *Lilium speciosum* is closely related to *L. auratum*. It, or any of its many hybrids is, and has been for some time, one of the most popular lilies for cut-flower use, and it lends itself readily to forcing. The stem grows to about five feet tall and carries several wide, spreading florets on long flower stalks. The segments have slightly wavy edges, gently reflexed, but not to the extent of a Turk's cap. The flower colour is usually white, with a pink stripe down the middle of each segment that becomes darker at the base. **Var.** *rubrum* (top left) has more deeply coloured flowers, and the clone **Album** has large, highly scented, pure white flowers. This lily flowers in late Summer and prefers a sunny position.

Lilium superbum (bottom right) is native to the Eastern and Central States of America, where its commonest vernacular name is **Swamp lily**. It was one of the first species of lily to be introduced from North America and is a plant that deserves its specific name: it produces stems up to eight feet tall with as many as 40 florets in the spike during July. The florets are of the Turk's cap type and are borne on longish individual stalks, which emerge horizontally and then curve gracefully downwards so that the flowers

nod gently. The florets are about four inches across with well-reflexed segments, which, when grown from seed, are usually in various shades of spotted orange – sometimes they are almost yellow and others are a mahogany-red. Although the plant enjoys a sunny situation, it likes its base to be kept shaded or damp.

The **Nankeen lily**, *L. × testaceum*, is regarded as the oldest recorded hybrid lily and is the product of *L. candidum* and *L. chalcedonicum*, a cross which has been

repeated several times and has produced offspring with surprisingly little variation from the original. It is a stunning plant that develops a purple stem with a
grey bloom, a good six feet tall, and carries up to 12 large flowers of a soft, warm,
apricot-colour with a few red spots. The segments of the individual florets are
open and flat, and spread to about four inches across: the top segments recurve
as the flower ages. It flowers just after mid-summer. Nowadays it is as rare as
hen's teeth, but, once again through the good offices of Martin Davis, we have
one bulb and will start the slow process of bulking up.

   Lilium longiflorum (left) is the dominant cut-flower lily of the florist's trade
and has pure white, six-inch-long, trumpet-shaped flowers. The plant is not long-
lived and therefore has to be restocked or regenerated regularly. The stems are
relatively short – only up to three feet in height – and carry about three or four
individual florets. It can be forced readily for spring use, but grown as an outdoor plant in Cornwall it flowers in July.

NARCISSUS

The genus **Narcissus** is a very large and diverse group of bulbous plants with an
extensive distribution throughout the warm temperate climates of the Northern
Hemisphere in the Old World, but with many outliers in colder climates – for
example, the Lent lily in the UK. The centre of diversity is in Iberia, where it
appears to be still evolving.

   The Victorians were enthusiastic about the cultivation of daffodils. By the mid-
nineteenth century, significant interspecific hybridization and selection had taken
place, an activity that accelerated rapidly into the twentieth century. Because of
their hardiness and the ease with which they can be cultivated, interest in the
breeding of the trumpet and the large- and small-cupped types was the most
rewarding. There was an enormous development during the twentieth century,
as enthusiastic fanciers and commercial breeders throughout the temperate
climates of the world expanded the potential and brought the genus to unprecedented levels of perfection, variety and form. Many thousands of cultivars were
registered over this period, with the result that genuinely old varieties are now
difficult to find and name with confidence. Because the major thrust of interest
has been in the trumpet and cup types, it is not surprising that only a handful of
nineteenth-century varieties can now be obtained at all readily. Relevant varieties
of other groups which have been less fashionable are much easier to source.

   Of the yellow trumpet varieties that can still be obtained, **King Alfred** (1899)
was an important and predominant member, but it is quickly losing ground as
it is no longer a significant commercial cut flower. However, it is still a useful
domestic variety because of its vigour and ability to tolerate pests and diseases.

Rows of early daffodils in the Flower Garden, 1995, the first year of cropping

Obvallaris, the Tenby daffodil, was still an important cut flower on the Isles of Scilly until the late 1950s. It is a short-stemmed, strong-growing, early-flowering selection with good yellow trumpets. It remains in commerce because of its ability to compete and colonize. **W.P. Milner** (1890) is a short (nine inches tall), small, trumpet, bicolour daffodil, equally at home as a cut flower or on the rock garden. Two other small but elegant yellow trumpet varieties are **Sir Watkin** and **Golden Spur**, both of which can still be found and identified, if only in hedgerows, where their robustness has allowed them to survive. We are actively seeking to recover a stock of each. Much the same could be said of **Princeps**, a bicolour trumpet of genuine nineteenth-century vintage.

Double-flowered forms were never common, but one of the oldest is **Butter and Eggs**, a short-stemmed, somewhat ragged double in two shades of golden-yellow, which dates from at least the eighteenth century. Nowadays it is generally found only in very old, undisturbed gardens. **Van Sion**, *N. telemonius plenus* is another old variety, and was effectively the first double-flowered form to be used as a commercial cut flower. It is a plant of medium vigour and somewhat ragged flower, but still fairly easy to obtain. **White Lady** (1898) is one of the few old,

small-cup varieties still to be found, and has recently been resurrected to commercial availability after it was saved from the hedgerow. It has a distinctly white perianth, and a very pale yellow cup fading to white.

The advantageous climate in the far South-west of England, especially in the Southern coastal strip, provides the mild Winters that the less hardy groups of narcissus (**Tazetta**, **Poetaz** and **Triandrus**) need, to be grown out-of-doors with confidence. A Head Gardener at Heligan during the late Victorian era would almost certainly have grown these types – if only to extend the season forwards without the necessity for forcing. Because of their limited use under outdoor conditions in most of Northern Europe, breeding and development of this group did not keep pace with that of the trumpet, cup, poeticus and jonquil types. Thus, despite the pressures of commercialization, with the consequent pursuit of improved varieties, very old cultivars

Cut flowers for a Friends' breakfast

can still be found reasonably easily. It is only in Cornwall and the Isles of Scilly that the most dramatic and least hardy group, the **Tazettas** (derived from *N. tazetta*), can be grown outside successfully. These produce their frost-susceptible leaves by November and generally flower early, producing multi-headed (polyanthus) stems of highly scented flowers in abundance from before Christmas and into March. The best-known of these cultivars, because of its extensive use as the basis of the commercial cut-flower industry in the Isles of Scilly, is **Soleil d'Or**. This variety is famous for its golden-yellow perianth, orange cup and strong, heady perfume. The best virus-free forms have eight or nine flowers per stem. The remainder of the commercial varieties in this group all have a white perianth: the best-known is **Paper White**, *N. tazetta papyraceus*. This has the potential for extreme precociousness of flowering – it probably produces the earliest flower of this group and even forces well. It has a white cup.

Gloriosus is an old, established, 'primitive' selection of *N. tazetta laticolor*. It has large, individual flowers with a pure white perianth and brilliant orange cup, and it is a vigorous grower. Also closely related is **N. canaliculatus**, a miniature sort growing to only nine inches in height. A group of very similar but nevertheless distinct varieties completes the picture. **Scilly White** has a pale, lemon-yellow cup and dark green leaves, and is one of the latest to flower. **Grand Monarque** has large flowers with broad petals and a neat, citron cup, persistent dark green leaves and a very vigorous and productive growth habit. **Grand Primo Citroniere** has a fairly tightly packed head of flowers with lemon-yellow cups. **Avalanche** (left) is a relatively new (1950s) name given to an old, unnamed stock grown on Tresco. It is an extraordinarily vigorous variety that has large, robust flowers with lemon-yellow cups on tall stems. It flowers late in the season and may be a sport of Scilly White. All of these varieties were taken into commercial cultivation in the 1870s, when T.A. Dorrien-Smith assembled as many variants of Tazettas as were available – some 70 in all – so that they could be assessed for suitability in the establishment of the cut-flower export industry that soon burgeoned on the Isles of Scilly. The only double form in this group currently, if not commonly, available is **Double Roman**, a double white with a citron centre.

The limited amount of breeding work involving the Tazettas was begun towards the end of the nineteenth century and chiefly revolved around crosses with forms of the **Poet's narcissus**, *N. poeticus*, producing the so-called **Poetaz types**. Among the early hybrids, which had greater hardiness and smaller stature, but retained the polyanthus flower and scent, was **Elvira**, which appeared in

1904. It had a white perianth and orange cup, and its claim to fame is the fact that its double sport, **Cheerfulness**, is a considerable commercial success. **Scarlet Gem**, with a yellow perianth and red cup, was introduced in 1910. It is a striking and beautiful variety, and is still grown today. Few, if any, of the other early Poetaz hybrids survive. The Poet's narcissus is also widely known as the **Pheasant's eye narcissus** and is generally the latest to flower. The variety **Recurvus**, with its slightly twisted and reflexed perianth, is the oldest form available, and **Ornatus**, another old variety with large flowers, can also be obtained commercially. The double form **Flore Pleno** is also readily found, but often as **albus plenus odoratus**. Varieties and hybrids of *N. triandrus* are generally of slightly later vintage, both **Thalia** and **Silver Chimes** being introduced in 1916.

The **jonquils** have a romantic association, largely because of their dainty habit and characteristic sweet fragrance. The conventional single jonquil, *N. jonquilla*, grows to about 18 ins. tall with an elegant stem and small yellow flowers. A very old double- flowered form known as **Queen Anne's Double** grows to 12 ins. tall and can still be found; but the usual double available commercially is the **Double Campernelle** (**odorus ruglosus plenus**) which is a hybrid with *N. odorus*. There are many fine jonquil hybrids available today, but they are virtually all of post-First World War vintage.

We grow a collection of narcissi in rows in the productive gardens to provide sweet-scented flowers for cutting in the very early Spring. Initially bulbs were planted in the Walled Garden, but these interfered with the sequence of cropping there for the rest of the year, as they had to be left in the ground for the leaves to die back. We now grow narcissi along the western border of the Vegetable Garden.

TULIP

Tulips were available throughout the nineteenth century, but we have not yet actively pursued any of the avenues which would allow us to source any of the relevant varieties. It is probable that we would focus on the old broken varieties, known, depending on their original categorization, as **Bybloems**, **Bizarres** and **Rembrandts**. However, these now rare forms are only obtainable from fanciers: they are not approved of by the EU (and therefore cannot be traded), as the characteristic breaking of the flower colour is caused by a virus.

CHAPTER 13
RHUBARB
CULTIVATION

Rhubarb, a peculiarly British crop, was much prized for dessert use during most of the nineteenth century. Highly productive, easy to grow and a nutritious food, its fall from grace can be attributed to it being grown in gardens and allotments by the 'working classes' during the early part of the twentieth century, when it became regarded as 'coarse'. The advent of cheap tinned peaches and the like finally killed off its use as a tasty dessert. But by the last quarter of the twentieth century the wheel had turned a full circle and rhubarb made a successful come-back as a fashionable and fairly expensive comestible, especially as the forced product. It has now become the principal component of many up-market cookery recipes. Several of the old varieties of rhubarb have stood the test of time in terms of their texture, flavour and colour, and many nineteenth-century varieties are still readily available.

Rhubarb is an undemanding crop to grow, requiring little more than a fertile, well-cultivated, freely draining but water-retentive soil and freedom from peren-nial weeds.

The crop is started from small crown pieces. These can be made by lifting old plants which have developed large woody crowns. The operation is carried out during the Winter by dividing them into smaller pieces after the leaves have died down. This involves taking off the peripheral groups of vigorous buds with a relevant healthy piece of the associated crown and discarding the woody centre. The pieces are replanted into a fresh bed at a spacing of five feet between the rows and three to four feet within the row. Woody crowns become less productive than young ones and should be divided every six years or so. The newly divided crowns should be established on a new site in order to minimize the build-up of potential crown rots. Waterlogging, caused by the soil becoming compacted, is probably the most common problem, and encourages the spread of fungi and bacteria liable to cause the crown to rot. Otherwise, the rhubarb crown is a tena-cious and vigorous specimen and will often survive long-term abandonment. In order to conserve soil moisture and help with weed control, the crop can be mulched with straw: this also eases compaction if the soil is wet when the crop

Kathy lifts a pot (page 199), and trims rhubarb stems (above)

is harvested. Because of the large amounts of vegetative material removed annually, rhubarb depletes the soil's reserves of nutrients, so attention should be paid to maintaining the fertility of the ground. If the crowns produce flower shoots, these should be pulled out in order to conserve the food supplies of the crown.

The premium crop of rhubarb is obtained by forcing during the early season, to produce the sought-after blanched leaf stalks. These are normally quite thin, and pale coral-pink in colour. The process requires warmth and darkness: this can be achieved by lifting crowns and bringing them into a suitable structure to be plunged into a small quantity of soil, as is done commercially, or by using forcing pots. These purpose-made, bell-shaped, terracotta pots are placed over the crowns during the late Winter. For the earliest season of cropping they are insulated on the outside with loose straw (top left). This practice of forcing the crop early in the season can be extended to eight or ten weeks in the garden, by covering a few crowns at a time, in succession, and by using an appropriate range of varieties. Forced crowns can be re-cropped later in the season as maincrops, after the crown has produced sufficient new leaves to support a crop being harvested; but care should be taken to ensure that the crown is allowed to rebuild its food reserves for the next season and another forced crop.

Few varieties survive from the nineteenth century, as it was quite common for rhubarb to be grown from seed: superior vegetative selections did not generally emerge until towards the end of the century.

VARIETIES

Timperley Early, an early flushing variety, produces strong, bright red, medium-thick sticks

during the Spring and Summer. These carry large, light green, fairly flat leaves. It responds well to forcing and, after a recovery period, continues to provide good crops of reasonable quality sticks through the maincrop season. It can also be used as a straightforward early-season crop. It has good texture, only developing stringiness if left beyond the fully expanded leaf stage. If there is room for only one variety of rhubarb, this is probably it.

Reed's Early Superb is an early flushing variety used for the earliest outdoor crop and the earliest forcing. As a normal outdoor crop it produces bright red, relatively thin sticks with good flavour and texture, so long as they are removed before they reach maturity, early in the season. However, it is principally a variety for forcing and under these conditions the sticks produced are slender, of medium length and good texture, and are a handsome pinky-red colour. It does not produce the highest quality sticks during the maincrop season, so is best left to build up reserves for next season's forcing.

Myatt's Victoria is perhaps the best-known and most commonly available of the traditional maincrop varieties of rhubarb. It produces prodigious crops of long, thick (sometimes huge), bright red sticks over an extensive season, and is recognizable by the large, crumpled leaves, which are a distinctive dark green. The flavour is the standard for rhubarb. The sticks should be harvested as they reach full size – if they are left any longer they become quite stringy.

Hawke's Champagne is regarded at Heligan as the 'class act' of the rhubarb beds: it has easily the best flavour, texture and colour of the varieties which we grow. It is essentially a maincrop variety, cropping throughout the Summer and providing substantial, but not heavy, yields. It develops handsomely coloured sticks of a bright coral-pink that mature to crimson and are quite slender. It can be forced at the end of the early season to extend the cropping period, when it produces equally good sticks of a beautiful pale coral-pink colour with excellent flavour. It was very popular as a commercial variety in late Victorian times.

At harvesting, the sticks of rhubarb are gently pulled out of the crown. If this proves difficult, pull them away from the crown, gently twisting them at the same time. They are trimmed by cutting the leaf virtually to its base, leaving only a token triangle of leaf blade. The base is left as pulled. Traditionally, the sticks are graded to uniform sizes and lengths and are then bundled and tied, top and bottom, with raffia. It does not take long for the sticks to flag and become limp, so they should be protected from excessive water loss. It is prudent to harvest only the younger sticks, thus leaving any older leaves to feed the crown. Try not to take more than half the sticks available at any one time. If terracotta forcing pots are not available, upturned oil drums, dustbins, or large buckets can be substituted.

CHAPTER 14

HERBS

In the context of this chapter, the term 'herb' is used in the narrow sense of a plant which is used for flavouring or colouring in various aspects of cooking and food preparation, although similar aromatic plants used for scenting products such as soap are included. The use of various plants for medicinal purposes is beyond our scope. Herbs, in our context generally, are those plants which exhibit a natural array of aromas, and so, in relatively small quantities, provide the cook with endless variations and nuances in flavouring a wide variety of dishes. Thus, although requiring only a relatively small area of land to produce much useful material, herbs have for long been a significant and integral part of the activities of both the head gardener and the cook. In the productive garden at Heligan, the cropping of herbs today is geared more to the requirements of our kitchen than to being particularly period-correct, in either type of plant or the quantity in which it is grown. The herbs used are still much the same as would have been available to the Victorians: it is the balance, in terms of quantity, which has probably changed most. It is worth pointing out that material from native plants, for all of these uses, was also collected from non-cultivated sources.

ANNUAL HERBS

Whatever the plant and whichever its season, the production process for annual herbs follows much the same pattern at Heligan. The required amount of seed is sown in a suitable-sized container and germinated in protection. When the seedlings are big enough to handle, they are pricked off into cellular trays at the equivalent of 24 or 40 per seed tray, depending on their size. Subsequently, they may be potted on, but all are eventually hardened off and planted out in their proper positions. If a particular plant or strain is required, it is usually possible to propagate it vegetatively.

Although **common thyme**, *Thymus vulgaris* (page 204), is, under normal conditions, a perennial plant, it is effectively grown in the kitchen garden as an annual. The earliest crop is started from seed sown early in the New Year. This provides the maincrop, and is used to maintain supplies through the Summer. A second crop is started in mid-summer. This is grown to enhance late-season

A corner of the Walled Garden, with thyme and golden marjoram, in rows

production, to take account of the quantities required for drying, and to provide relatively good quality material over the Winter and in the very early part of the following season. **Lemon-scented thyme**, *Thymus citriodorus*, can be treated in exactly the same way as common thyme, but is normally required in much smaller quantities.

Parsley, although nominally a biennial, is grown as an annual herb. It is probably the most important leaf crop to be grown in the kitchen garden and was/is required for all sorts of flavouring and decorative purposes in the preparation of food for the table. The earliest crop is sown in the New Year. Patience is the watchword, as parsley seed is notoriously slow to germinate. Because of the need for regular supplies of leaves in significant quantities, regular successive sowings

Cut herbs: thyme, chives and parsley (above). Golden marjoram (below)

need to be made. The plants have only a limited productive life and tend to bolt after mid-summer. The earliest crop is grown in the Walled Garden, and the maincrop in the Vegetable Garden. The principal type grown is **Moss triple-curled** (or similar), although nowadays there is an increasing demand for 'plain' or flat-leaved parsley, on the potentially spurious basis that it has superior flavour. We grow two flat-leaved types – **French** and **Italian**. If there is space to leave some bolted plants to mature, seed can be harvested and is also used for flavouring, especially cheese dishes.

The various **marjorams** (see start of chapter and above) and **oreganos** are particularly fashionable at the moment, due to the vogue for Mediterranean influences in cooking. **Pot marjoram** and **oregano** are technically perennials but are

treated as annuals, and **sweet marjoram** is an annual. All of these are grown in moderate quantities. To keep the productivity of sweet marjoram high, a second crop is grown for the late season.

Coriander was grown for its seeds in the nineteenth century, for use as a flavouring. Although coriander seed is still used, the current demand is for the leaf and stalks for use as a green herb – again, a flight of fashion while the various types of Oriental cooking are in vogue. The plant grown to provide this crop is traditionally known as **cilantro**. To maintain supplies of good quality a second crop will be needed. Virtually the same comments apply to **dill**, the seeds of which were produced for flavouring, especially in the pickling of gherkins. The requirement today, however, is principally for the green product.

Chervil, which is available in both **plain** and **curled** forms, is grown exclusively as a green herb and is now used for salads as well as for flavouring oil-based dressings. It is a crop which needs successional sowing and harvesting while it is young, in order to maintain high-quality leaves with good flavour. Generally we direct-sow this crop and then thin it if necessary.

Summer savory (top left) is treated as an annual and develops into what is virtually a small sub-shrub. It is probably the least known and used of this group. It has a very distinctive and pleasant flavour, and was traditionally used as the herb boiled with broad beans (in the same way that mint is used with peas). It requires more space per plant than the average herb and is planted at 15 ins. or so apart.

Pot marigold is the distinctive, annual, orange-yellow-flowered marigold. It is so tenacious that it sows itself: seedlings can be lifted in the Spring and planted in the allocated row. It is a colourful plant with a long flowering season, which justifies it a corner in the kitchen garden. The flowers were used to colour stews and gravies.

Basil (bottom left) is about the least hardy of all the annual leaf herbs that we grow. Its soft green leaves, with their evocative aroma, are well known, and although used in a variety of guises are chiefly associated with enhancing the appeal of tomatoes and to make pesto sauce. It was widely used in English cooking, but lost popularity through the twentieth century, only to regain currency with the vogue for Italian and other Mediterranean recipes. In order to get a crop by mid-summer it is necessary to sow the seed under glass in late March so that it can be planted out in late April or after the frosts have passed. The crop should be harvested when quite young, and well before it runs to flower. Successive sowings can be made from May onwards by direct-drilling, and a late sowing can be made in pots to provide some shoots over the Winter. In order to obtain the maximum aroma it should be grown in a well-drained, very sunny, warm position.

The Victorians would have been familiar with only one or two types of basil and would, no doubt, be surprised at the huge range available today.

Fennel (right) is another Mediterranean annual with a very distinctive aroma, which has become naturalized in many places – indeed, one of my abiding memories of childhood in the Isles of Scilly is the ubiquitous scent of fennel during the Summer. It is not a herb with many culinary uses, being employed chiefly in fish dishes and as a garnish, but we also use it as cut foliage. We grow a few plants of the common or **green** type and the same amount of the **bronze-leaved** form. The few plants we need are raised in the usual way and planted out in a row in the herb border. It is prudent not to let the plants set seed: if these get scattered, all germinate the next year in places where they are not wanted.

The mint bed in the Melon Yard

PERENNIAL HERBS

The various perennial herbs that we grow do not fit easily into a regular pattern of production, so tend to be sited in a semi-permanent area or confined to an individual station, particularly if they have a propensity to be invasive.

The various types of **mint** are used for a variety of culinary purposes, mainly as infused flavourings in boiling various vegetables, for mint sauce and as garnishes, but also, in today's high-powered kitchens, in oil-based dressings. **Spearmint** is the traditional garden variety, with smooth-surfaced, somewhat spear-shaped, mid-green leaves that have the correct flavour for mint sauce, although there are several similar smooth-leaved types which work perfectly well. It is generally agreed that either **apple mint** or **Bowles mint** is the best to use to infuse the cooking water of peas and potatoes, etc. Both of these varieties have large, roundish, thick, light grey-green, distinctly hairy leaves. For those who wish to make mint tea, we grow **Moroccan mint**, which has smooth, mid-green, narrow leaves. These are lightly diced and then infused in the fresh condition to make the drink. In order to provide a variety of scents for the visitor to experience, we also grow

peppermint, which is suffused with a dark purple colour to its leaves and stems, and the similar **red pea mint**, which is suffused with a more reddish colour but is also predominantly peppermint-flavoured, although coarser in its aromatics; and **eau-de-Cologne mint**, **lavender mint**, **orange mint** and **pineapple mint**, the names of which are self-explanatory.

All of the mints are stoloniferous in habit and, once established, are capable of running riot through the area provided for them and then invading adjacent plots. They must therefore be rigorously constrained and kept within bounds: growing them in some kind of container is probably the safest method. Propagation is simply by extracting some runners just as growth is beginning in the Spring, and replanting them in the required site. It is also quite feasible to propagate plants from cuttings. In order to keep them in productive condition, the plants should be cut down regularly to keep new, clean, vigorous vegetative

Herbs in the Flower Garden: sages (foreground) and rosemary (behind)

shoots coming. If mint is required in the Winter, runners can be lifted, potted up and forced in the greenhouse. Our mints have been, and still are, grown in a bed in front of the potting shed, but despite our best efforts they quickly get mixed, so we have resorted to growing them in tubs as well.

Rosemary is a sub-shrub originating from around the Mediterranean basin, and was probably introduced to this country by the Romans. It is a plant that has given rise to more myths and legends associated with its use than most. It can develop to relatively large proportions, and in order to control its size and maintain its productivity in the garden it should be pruned regularly each year, as a severe pruning back into old wood will generally not produce regeneration. There are many different provenances which provide several nuances of flavour – depending largely on the levels of the 'pine' note in the balance of aromatics – although this factor does not yet seem to have percolated to the kitchen. The type from the South of France was the traditional plant to be grown for culinary purposes. It is characterized by large, broad, dark green leaves, often with a white indumentum on the young shoots, and pale slate-blue flowers. An erect

form, **Miss Jessupp's Upright**, was introduced by E.A. Bowles at the start of the twentieth century, but the material offered under the name today is rarely, if ever, this plant. Forms with finer and smaller leaves and darker blue or pink flowers originate from various Mediterranean islands and generally have a much higher pine component in their aromatics. Among its non-culinary uses, rosemary's commonest application is in hair preparations such as shampoos.

Lavender is not generally used in cooking, usually being employed in making cosmetic preparations or being dried for use in lavender bags and suchlike. Its use depends on the level and type of aromatics (lavender oil) present, and nowadays it is prudent to use one of the commercial varieties used for oil extraction rather than the traditional, billowing, cottage-garden type, **Vera**. Such varieties are available on the amateur market.

Sage is another of the highly aromatic sub-shrubs from the Mediterranean basin. Typically, it has wrinkled, velvety, grey-green leaves and a somewhat low-growing, woody habit. Its aromatics are dramatically enhanced when it is grown in a well-drained, sunny position, where it is marginally under stress. It will, of course, grow more luxuriantly and productively in good soil and typical kitchen-garden conditions, but some of the aromatics will be lost. Sage is readily propagated from cuttings taken in the Autumn and rooted in a cold frame over the Winter. Rooted cuttings are planted out into rows two feet apart, at 15-ins. intervals. If there is no access to cutting material, plants can be raised from seed. There are a number of variants: one with narrow leaves used to be considered superior in flavour to other varieties, but most types are

Variegated sage (above); purple sage (below)

not lacking in this respect and are more than adequate. (A broad-leaved form is apparently preferred by sausage makers.) There are ornamental varieties available which are equally aromatic: **Purpurascens** has purple leaves, **Tricolor** has leaves variegated white and pink on purple, and **Icterina** has yellow-variegated leaves. Sage is often dried, and leaves for this treatment are traditionally harvested at flowering time.

Tansy is a native plant and has a very limited use. The leaves are used in the flavouring of traditional, old English pudding recipes for Easter and the like. Tansy is a perennial that grows to three feet in height, and one plant in the garden is more than adequate. If for nothing else, its large, flat, yellow flowers during the Summer make it worth the space.

Bergamot, *Monnarda didyma*, is of only marginal significance as a herb, the fresh leaves of which are infused to make Oswego tea, a native North American drink. However, it is so decorative and aromatic that it is worth having a few plants, even if only as a whimsy!

Tarragon is used traditionally as a flavouring for vinegar, although it was used in small quantities in cooking – in stews and omelettes, in the flavourings for pickles and as fresh leaves in salads. In France it is one of the fines herbes. The plant known as **French tarragon** is the particular species needed. This is a perennial sub-shrub which reaches four or five feet in height if left untouched. In the garden, regular removal of the shoots keeps it more compact. Normally grown on a semi-permanent site, together with other shrubby herbs, probably only one plant is necessary. French tarragon is propagated readily from tip cuttings taken

once the new flush of spring growth has settled down. The plant should have a productive life of three or four years before being replaced. It should not be confused with **Russian tarragon**, which is treated as an annual, is grown from seed and has an altogether coarser flavour.

Horseradish can rapidly become an invasive weed, but growing it gives the means to make fresh horseradish sauce, a benefit that makes the effort of constraining it worthwhile. Horseradish is propagated by root cuttings at any time of the year: take vigorous, current-season's roots about four to six inches long and insert them, vertically and the right way up, in the required cropping position. They grow vigorously unless conditions are exceptionally harsh. Be aware, however, that in lifting material for use, pieces of root will be left *in situ* and tend to regenerate. The same is true for any discarded pieces of root, which usually establish themselves where they are left, so the plant is best confined to an isolated corner.

Chive is one of the green-leaved herb crops that will probably be used regularly and in fairly large quantities during the course of the year: the 'grass' is used for flavouring soups, omelettes and salads and as a garnish. This relative of the onion is a short-term perennial which increases by continually dividing its crown shoots. However, as with most of these short-term perennials, it is best treated as an annual in order to maintain quality and productivity. Mature clumps should be lifted from the previous season's beds during the Spring and divided into small groups of healthy, vigorous individuals. The leaves of these new plants are trimmed back to about half their length to reduce water loss and then planted in the new site at 12 ins. between the rows and six inches between the plants. A second renewal should be carried out in the early Autumn to produce a new bed that will crop from late in the same season round to the following Autumn. With heavy cropping, a bed of chives can be expected to yield productively for only up to a year: production is therefore a continuous cycle of renewal on two separate time-scales.

Lemon balm is hardly a culinary herb but the aromatics of its leaves, which were used traditionally to add a fragrance to soap, make it worth a corner. However, it can be invasive, so bear this in mind when choosing a site for it.

A few other herbs find their way into our borders in small quantities to fulfil various needs. The annual, self-seeding **borage** is grown for its intense cobalt-blue flowers – so necessary to finish the decoration on a glass of Pimms. The sub-shrub **southernwood** is grown as a representative *Artemisia*. When we manage to germinate them, we also grow **angelica** and **lovage**. Still others have no real justification other than the fact that we like them and they are decorative: **pineapple sage** (left) is a good example.

CHAPTER 15

A MISCELLANY OF VEGETABLES-CUM-FRUITS

All the fruits treated here – and, strictly speaking, they are fruits – are usually regarded as vegetables and found under that category in seed catalogues.

TOMATOES, AUBERGINES AND PEPPERS

This group of half-hardy, annual, fruit-cum-vegetable crops is chiefly grown and sited on an *ad hoc* basis in the garden: the plants are put out in any suitable situation that happens to become vacant and needs a tenant for the Summer. The major formal thrust, however, occurs in the Citrus House, when it has been vacated by the trees for the duration of the Summer. This otherwise empty glasshouse is used to grow a selection of these plants, which are managed individually in large pots. We grow a whole range of varieties from this group of crops, with no particular reference to them having to be period-correct. They represent one of our collective whimsies, and the selection varies from year to year. Sylvia grows what she fancies: many of the varieties *are* period-correct, but the only criterion for selection is that they are interesting for our visitors in one way or another and provide us with a variety of flavours.

Tomatoes, peppers and aubergines are all propagated and grown on much the same system. The seeds are sown in half seed trays or pots, depending on the quantities required, and placed in the heated propagating frame during March. When germination has occurred the seedlings are pricked off (at the cotyledon stage) into cellular trays at a spacing equivalent to 20 in a seed tray. When big enough, they are potted on into size 60 terracotta pots and grown on in a warm and light position on the back shelves in the Melon House. If progress is good they may be potted on into 48s. From there they move to their final positions, having been hardened off as required. Virtually all the varieties are grown as single-stem, upright cordons, tied to a cane, either in the ground or in large (ten-inch or larger) terracotta pots. They have their side shoots removed to maintain the cordon shape, but specifically bushy types are, of course, allowed to grow freely.

Over the years we have accumulated seed of the following varieties, and in any one season the selection is made from these together with any new interests. If the plants are sufficiently isolated from others when they flower, we can eventually collect and save seed. In order to be on the safe side, tomatoes, for instance, require a separation of 15 ft. from other varieties to minimize the likelihood of cross-pollination. Seed-saving in these crops is quite straightforward. Separate the seeds from the fully ripe fruits and leave them in some warm water overnight: any remaining pulp will ferment and can be separated from the seeds by decanting off the detritus – the seeds sink and the detritus floats. Then wash and rinse the seeds to provide a clean sample, and finally leave them in a 10 per cent solution of washing soda until they are no longer sticky and separate easily. Then rinse them again and dry on absorbent paper – tabloid newsprint is ideal! The seeds are then stored in a dry, airtight jar: viability is maintained for several years. Tomatoes certainly need this treatment, but peppers and aubergines may not be quite sticky enough to warrant the washing-soda component of the process.

TOMATO VARIETIES

Banana Legs is a compact plant; very prolific over a long season. Its bright yellow, pointed, banana-shaped fruits grow to about four inches long and just over an inch across. The flavour is meaty.

Black Russian (**Black Krim**, top right), from the Black Sea region, has large fruits of unusual, deep, shiny, black-red colour with green shoulders; internally it is reddish-green. It is very sweet, and an early cropper.

Elberta Girl is a bushy plant, named because of its similarity in colouring to the famous Elberta peach. The plum-shaped fruits are red striped with gold.

Gold Nugget is a vigorous, compact, bushy plant up to about 24 ins. in height. It fruits early and prolifically, bearing sweet, small (one inch in diameter) oval fruits with a good flavour.

Golden Sunrise (page 215) is a well-known, old yellow variety with regular, globular fruits about two

inches in diameter. It is an early, heavy cropper, and the fruit has a sweet flavour.

Green Zebra (top left) is best grown in the greenhouse as it needs a long season. It produces green fruits with blackish stripes, which have an excellent flavour.

Mini Orange is a large, bushy plant. It produces huge crops of sweet, brilliant orange fruits, each one and a half inches in diameter, in clusters of five.

Pink Brandywine is a typical potato-leafed, Brandywine type, of the Amish. Its huge pink fruits have few seeds and are famous for their flavour.

Pink Ping-pong has pink, sweet, cherry-type fruits up to two inches in diameter.

Riesentraube (bottom right) is an old German variety which produces massive clusters of small, red, pear-shaped fruits with good flavour.

Silvery Fir Tree is a bush with fern-like foliage and small, red, beefsteak-type fruits.

Tangella, derived from Ailsa Craig, has round, two-inch diameter fruits with a brilliant orange skin. The fruits are even and uniform, with clear, yellowish flesh with good flavour.

Tigerella (mid left), a variety from the 1960s bred by Lou Darby at the Glasgow Crops Research Institute (GCRI), bears smallish (up to two-inch) fruits, striped red and yellow, which have a rich tangy flavour. The yields are heavy.

Tiger Tom (bottom left), another variety bred by the legendary Lou Darby, has smallish, round fruits, striped brown and yellow.

AUBERGINE VARIETIES

Apple Green (page 218, top right) has very small (about one inch in diameter) round to oval, green fruits, whose flesh is sweet. It is productive and compact.

Black Beauty (*c.* 1875; page 218, mid left) is an old variety with large (six- to eight-inch), deep purple-black, oval to egg-shaped, glossy fruits.

Long Purple, a variety dating from the first half of the nineteenth century, has six-inch-long, pear-shaped, deep violet fruits.

Skoutari (next page, bottom) is very similar in description to the old Guadeloupe of Vilmorin. The long fruits (up to about eight inches) are slightly pear-shaped, violet irregularly striped with white, and second-early.

Turkish Orange has small, roundish, but irregularly shaped fruits that turn orange when mature, and bitter: eat them green.

Violetta di Firenze (mid right) bears large, heavy, round to oval fruits whose rose-coloured skin has white blotches overlaid with violet. It is a productive plant.

White Egg (top left) is a Japanese variety producing small, oval, white fruits, the size and shape of a bantam's egg, which eventually turn yellow when fully ripe. The flavour is spicy.

SWEET PEPPER VARIETIES

Bull's Horn Red has narrow, irregularly tapering (from over two inches), somewhat curved, red fruit up to about six inches long, which are aromatic and have a sweet flavour. It requires a warm Summer, so is best grown in the greenhouse.

Bull's Horn Yellow, as above, but yellow.

Bull-nosed Red (**Sweet Mountain**) is a very old, conventional bell pepper producing brilliant red fruits.

Luteus is an old bell pepper with shortish, glossy, yellow fruits.

A harvest of aubergines, tomatoes, chillies and sweet peppers

FRUITS TREATED IN SIMILAR FASHION

OKRA

Okra, also known as Lady's Fingers or Gumbo, depending on where you are in the subtropics, was a plant known to the Victorians, but it is doubtful that it had wide popularity, despite being mentioned regularly in the standard texts. In our situation it only performs satisfactorily if grown in the greenhouse in a pot, tied to a cane, and is integrated into the management of this group of crops. It is propagated and raised in the manner detailed above. In order to ensure a crop we grow a modern F1 hybrid, **Pure Luck**.

PHYSALIS

Nowadays the Cape gooseberry is a regular feature on the supermarket shelves, for use in fruit salads and the like. *Physalis edulis* is the usual variety – an almost shrubby, highly branched plant, up to three feet tall and with a similar spread.

The overgrown Melon House (above), for raising cucurbits, with horseshoe boiler (below)

It produces its papery calyx pods with the fleshy, golden-orange, cherry-sized, globular fruits hidden inside. It is grown outside in a sunny border, after having been raised as a pot-grown plant under glass, from a spring sowing. It grows vigorously and crops prolifically, the fruit ripening by about September in a normal season. The variety **P. pubescens** is slightly smaller and hairier, and is reputed to have a better flavour. In continental catalogues the Cape gooseberry sometimes appears as **P. peruviana**. We also attempt to grow a second species, **Physalis ixocarpa**, which produces fruits of a violet colour, although those we have grown so far look more like, and are more the size of, the **Toma Verde** of Mexico – perhaps our seed was incorrectly named. The latter fruits are used in Mexico as a constituent of salsas. Whatever our plant is, it hardly manages to ripen its prolific crop of fruits in an outdoor situation in Cornwall.

Tim Smit views the derelict Melon House (above); the restored Melon House (right)

CUCURBITS

INDOOR CUCUMBERS

The principal crop of cucumbers is grown in the first segment of the Melon House as a series of single-cordon plants trained up and across the horizontal wires in the roof. The crop is grown as if it were unheated, so is planted out at the beginning of May. An earlier crop could be achieved, but the greenhouse space is more valuable for plant-raising during the early season. The seeds are sown in late March in cellular trays and germinated in the heated propagation box. As soon as the cotyledons have emerged, the seedlings are potted on into size 60 pots, in which they are planted deeply. When they have filled these pots they are potted on into 48s, and again are planted deeply so that the plants can root up the stem and so provide greater anchorage and stability during the subsequent cropping cycle. In late April the bench in the greenhouse is filled with a ten-inch-deep layer of well-rotted spent manure from the heating pits of the pineapple

Cucumbers growing in the Melon House (above). Cut cucumber (below)

frame. This is topped with about three inches of coarsely sieved topsoil taken from across the Vegetable Garden. In early May, when this base has warmed up, the seedlings are planted along the front wall of the house at 18-ins. intervals and are tied to a cane, which is also attached to the lowest wire in the roof. The plants establish themselves quickly and soon climb up the cane and into the roof of the house where they are trained, as single stems, on the underside of the wires. Side shoots are removed and a pair of fruits is taken from each node. These hang down from the roof, so grow straight and are easily harvested. This is an extremely productive method that answers our need for plenty of fruits in quick succession. In order to take a maximum crop efficiently, we use a modern female

F1 hybrid variety such as **Femdam**, rather than the less sophisticated, period-correct types such as **Telegraph**. We have used the latter, but prefer to get maximum bang for our bucks (and effort). The plants develop and crop quickly, reaching the ridge of the house by July. We follow this crop with a second, sown in June and planted out as soon as the previous crop is cleared, which continues to produce fruit into late September.

The chief problem is caused by red spider mite, but the incidence of this pest is significantly reduced by maintaining a damp atmosphere within the house and using predators for biological control. In prolonged damp, sunless, cool conditions, fungal blossom end rots can occur: we tend to trust in our own individual gods and wear flannel next the skin as a method of control – that is, we hope the conditions improve quickly!

OUTDOOR CUCUMBERS

Other crops of cucumber are grown in the original cold frames of the Melon Yard (next page), and provide the much hardier ridge, gherkin and globe types (right). These are all propagated and grown on in the same way, concurrently with the crop described above. They are planted out at about two plants to an English light in a cold frame that has been prepared in advance by double digging. The lights are left on the frame, with permanent airing, until about the end of May when they are removed altogether. The cucumbers are then left to wander where they wish – although we do tend to prune them to shape if they overflow the frame. In general, cropping of all the types is prolific.

RIDGE CUCUMBER

Bedfordshire Prize Ridge is a selection of a very old, ribbed cucumber. The fruit is almost cylindrical and has a few small spines on the ribs. It is best harvested when the fruits are about six to eight inches long. It has dense, crisp flesh, but is best peeled before eating: the skin is both rough and somewhat bitter.

GLOBE CUCUMBER

Crystal Apple (right) is an apple-shaped cucumber about two and a half inches in diameter, with a creamy white skin. **Lemon** is an old variety with fruit of about the size and shape of large lemons, with yellow skins and tangy flavour. Both are good novelties for children.

GHERKIN (CORNICHON)

Paris Pickling (**Vert Petit de Paris**), a nineteenth-century French variety, produces short, stubby, spiny fruits. It is extraordinarily prolific. The dill seed crop is grown particularly for use in the pickling of these fruit.

MELONS IN THE MELON HOUSE

The crop of melons is grown in the middle segment of the Melon House, chiefly because it is warmer than elsewhere, and partly because if things go wrong it's less obvious! However, we have now just about cracked the traditional growing of melons and can produce very acceptable crops. From the 2004 season we are growing the melons in the end segment so that any errors will be on view. We are currently growing the crop without heat, although we are gradually installing a heating system. As with the cucumber crop, we do not start the melons too early: the space is more valuable to us for raising other plants, and the melons benefit from the late start as they only thrive in the warmer summer temperatures. The crop is managed in the same fashion as the cucumbers – as a series of single cordons at two feet apart – which means we can grow eight plants in the house.

In Victorian times the culture of melons in a heated greenhouse was a high art, and crops were harvested from early April onwards. The recommendations for the methods of training were legion, but we try to grow the plants as simple single cordons, a method allowing us to grow more than one variety. The process for growing this crop was devised originally by Paul Haywood. In recent years it was refined to our now successful crop yields by Johanna, and Sylvia is taking the process forward. The following description is derived from Johanna's notes:

> The seeds are sown, in heated conditions, on or about the first day of May. They germinate within a few days and the seedlings are grown on in the same way as cucumbers. They are planted out into beds at the very beginning of June, a foot from the greenhouse wall, on little mounds to avoid water splashing on to the stems during watering – melons are particularly prone to stem rot. They are trained to a cane and when they reach the height of the first wire the leader is cut back to leave two side shoots, one of which is trained as the new leader. As this leader is trained up the roof

wires each of its laterals are cut back to four leaves, or two leaves after a flower and ultimately a potential fruit. The other potential leader is removed once the progress of the other is assured. As a rule of thumb, when three female flowers are open at the same time they are receptive and can be pollinated. A male flower is cut when the anthers are dehiscing and liberating pollen. It is rubbed on the stigmas of the female flowers when conditions are sunny, otherwise the pollen forms a sticky lump. When all the pollinated flowers have set fruit and these have reached golf-ball size, the crop is thinned to between four and six fruits per plant, depending on variety. When these fruits have reached the size of an apple, each is supported with a cotton net tied to the wire. The plants are watered only with warm water. The atmosphere of the greenhouse is kept moist while the fruit is developing and swelling but is then maintained at a drier regime as the fruit is ripening. The ripeness of melons of this type can be gauged by looking at the junction of the stalk and the fruit: when the disc begins to lift from the fruit, it is time to pick for optimum harvest.

We have the seed sources to grow four varieties, but which we grow depends on which plants are strongest at planting time.

Blenheim Orange is a very early English variety. The fruit is a very slightly flattened globular shape, six inches in diameter and marginally locular in outline. It has a smooth, pale, glaucous skin, which develops a slightly orange tinge and has green lines delineating the locules when ripe. The flesh is fragrant, orange-red and sweet, the seed cavity is relatively small and packed with seeds, and the fruits are very aromatic. It was used to crop at any season, but under our system is the second variety to mature.

Charentais is a typical, traditional, French Canteloupe melon. The smooth-skinned fruits are spherical with slight ovalling to both ends, five inches in diameter, and have a locular appearance. They ripen early to a golden-yellow, with the locular lines remaining blue-green. The sweet, fragrant flesh is bright orange.

Emerald Gem has the largest fruits of the varieties we grow, at least seven inches long by six inches wide. The fruits are an even oval to round shape, and have smooth, shiny, mottled green skins with light beige netting. The green flesh is sweet and aromatic. We grow this variety from home-saved seed.

Hero of Lockinge is a mid-nineteenth century variety that was very popular in its day. Of the melons we grow, this is the earliest to mature. Due to its susceptibility to stem rot, it is a tricky subject, but we manage to produce fruit and grow the plants from home-saved seed. The fruits are large, almost globular but

Paul harvests and tastes Hero of Lockinge in the Melon House (left), celebrating the peak of summer harvest. Gardeners' Notes (above) remind us of the ongoing cycle of seasonal activity in the productive gardens, now re-established by the team at Heligan

slightly flattened, and the yellow skin has a light beige netting over the whole surface. The flesh is white, very fragrant and sweet, and the plants are capable of high yields.

We also have seed of other old varieties, such as **Blackrock** and **Pineapple**, but only use them very occasionally, just to keep the seed stock going.

BIBLIOGRAPHY

This list aims to indicate the range of sources we have used to help inform our progress. These and many other volumes are retained in the library at Heligan as a resource for staff, and for other interested parties to consult by arrangement. We have several of the most significant titles in various editions, enabling us to build up a picture of how thought, comprehension and technique progressed in this area of activity. A second source of information is provided by nurserymen's catalogues, and we retain all the catalogues we use from year to year. This list is only a selection which is relevant to the subject-matter of this volume.

GENERAL

Anderson, J. (c.1871), *The New Practical Gardener*. Glasgow, Edinburgh and London: William MacKenzie.

Bagenal, N.B. (1939), *Fruit Growing: Modern Cultural Methods*. London and Melbourne: Ward Lock & Co.

Barron, A.F. (1900), *Vines and Vine Culture*. 4th edn. London: Journal of Horticulture Office.

Bean, W.J. (1980), *Trees and Shrubs Hardy in the British Isles*. 8th edn. London: John Murray.

Brooke, J. (1951), *Peaches, Apricots and other Stone Fruits*. London: Faber & Faber.

Bryan, J.E. (2002), *Bulbs*. Revised edn. Portland, Oregon: Timber Press.

Bultitude, J. (1983), *Apples*. London: Macmillan Press.

Bunyard, E.A. (1925), *A Handbook of Hardy Fruits, More Commonly Grown in Great Britain*. 2 vols. London: John Murray.

Bunyard, G. & Thomas, O. (1904), *The Fruit Garden*. London: Country Life & George Newnes.

Burbidge, F.W. (1877), *Cultivated Plants: Their Propagation and Improvement*. Edinburgh and London: William Blackwood & Sons.

Choisel, J-L. (1991), *Guide des Pommes de Terroir à la Table*. Paris: Editions Hervas.

Cook, E.T. (ed.) (c. 1900), *The Century Book of Gardening*. London: Country Life & George Newnes.

Delbard, G. (1947), *Les Beaux Fruits de France*. Paris: Editions Delbard.

Grubb, N.H. (1949), *Cherries*. London: Crosby Lockwood & Son.

Hyams, E. (1949), *The Grape Vine in England*. London: Faber & Faber.

Johnson, G.W. (1846), *A Dictionary of Modern Gardening*. London: Robert Baldwin.

— (1860), *The Cottage Gardeners' Dictionary*. 5th edn. London: W. Kent & Co.

Loudon, J.C. (1822), *Encyclopaedia of Gardening*. London: Longman.

M'Intosh, C. (1847), *The Flower Garden*. New edn. London: W.S. Orr & Co.

— (1853), *The Book of the Garden*. 2 vols. Edinburgh and London: William Blackwood & Sons.

Mawe, T. and Abercrombie, J., *Gardener's Calendar*. 9th edn., 1782; 18th edn., 1805. London.

Morgan, J. & Rogers, A. (1993), *The Book of Apples*. London: Ebury Press.

Nicholson, G. (1887), *The Illustrated Dictionary of Gardening*. London: L. Upcott Gill.

Pearson, R.H. (ed.), various dates; early twentieth-century, *Present Day Gardening*. London and Edinburgh: T.C. & E.C. Jack.

Roach, F.A. (1985), *Cultivated Fruits of Britain: Their Origin and History*. Oxford: Blackwell.

Roberts, H. (ed.), various dates; early twentieth-century, *Handbooks of Practical Gardening*. Thirty-eight titles on individual subjects by specialist authors. London and New York: John Lane, The Bodley Head.

Robinson, W. (1875), *Hardy Flowers*. New edn. London: Frederick Warne & Co.

— (1883), *The English Flower Garden*. 8th edn., 1900; 10th edn, 1906. London: John Murray.

— (1893), *Hardy Flowers*. 5th edn. London: The Garden.

Roe, E.P. (1880), *Success with Small Fruits*. London: Selley, Jackson, & Halliday.

Sanders, T.W. & Lansdell, J. (1924), *Grapes, Peaches and Melons and How to Grow Them*. London: W.H. & L. Collingridge.

Saunt, J. (2000), *Citrus Varieties of the World*. Norwich: Sinclair.

Scott, J. (late nineteenth century), *The Orchardist*. 2nd edn. of the catalogue of Scott's of Merriot. Somerset.

Speechley, W. (1821), *A Treatise on the Culture of the Vine*. 3rd edn. London: Longman, Hurst, Rees, Orme & Brown.

— (1821), *A Treatise on the Culture of the Pineapple*. 3rd edn. London: Longman, Hurst, Rees, Orme & Brown.

Spiers, V. (1996), *Burcombes, Queenies and Colloggetts*. St Dominic, Cornwall: West Brendon Press.

Taylor, H.V. (1936), *The Apples of England*. London: Crosby Lockwood & Son.

— (1949), *Plums*. London: Crosby Lockwood & Son.

Thompson, R. (1851), *The Gardener's Assistant*. Glasgow and Edinburgh: Blackie & Son. (This treatise ran to several editions and revisions and eventually was edited by William Watson [2 vols, 1902]. The last edition was published as six volumes in 1925, entitled *Watson's Gardener's Assistant*.)

Thomson, D. (1881), *Fruit Culture under Glass*. 2nd edn. Edinburgh and London: William Blackwood & Sons.

Thomson, W. (1875), *A Practical Treatise on the Cultivation of the Grape Vine*. 8th edn. Edinburgh and London: William Blackwood & Sons.

Weathers, J. (ed.) (1913), *Commercial Gardening*. 4 vols. London: The Gresham Publishing Co.

Wood, S. (1876), *A Plain Guide to Good Gardening*. 2nd edn. London: Crosby Lockwood & Co.

Wright, J. (c. 1900), *The Fruit Growers Guide*. 6 vols. London: J.S. Virtue & Co.

Wright, W.P. (1913), *Cassell's Dictionary of Practical Gardening*. 2 vols. London, New York, Toronto and Melbourne: Cassell & Co.

ROYAL HORTICULTURAL SOCIETY YEAR BOOKS

We have the majority of the numbers, but the sets are still incomplete. Of particular interest in the context of this book are the following titles: *Daffodil and Tulip*, *Lily* and *Fruit*.

The standard manual on growing fruit is *The Fruit Garden Displayed* (1st edn. 1951), published by the RHS.

MAFF BULLETINS

Many of these publications have a section at the end devoted to gardens, and represent an interesting window on the past. The date shown is usually for the first edition: after the Second World War, most titles were revised fairly regularly until the 1970s.

Number	Date	Title
4	1930	*Bush Fruits*
65	1933	*Crop Production in Frames*
77	1934	*Tomatoes*
95	1937	*Strawberries*
96	1936	*Commercial Flower Production Part 1*
110	1938	*Commercial Flower Production Part 3*
112	1939	*Commercial Flower Production Part 4*
119	1939	*Plums and Cherries*
125	1945	*Culinary Herbs and their Cultivation*
133	1946	*Apples and Pears*
156	1955	*Cane Fruits*
197	1967	*Flowers from Bulbs and Corms*
Technical Bulletin 26	1973	*Flowering Periods of Tree and Bush Fruits*

SUPPLIERS

The nurseries and seedhouses listed below happen to be the suppliers that we have contacted and from whom we have received efficient service and co-operation. There are, of course, many other reliable suppliers, and this list is by no means exclusive. Because we are sited in Cornwall there tends to be a bias to West-country suppliers: we aim to encourage support for local businesses.

FLOWERS AND BULBS

Chase Organics Ltd., Riverdene Estate, Molesey Road, Hersham, Surrey KT12 4RG. *Flower seeds*

Cotswold Garden Flowers, Sandy Lane, Badsey, Evesham, Worcestershire WR11 5EZ. *Gladiolus and herbaceous plants*

De Jager & Sons, The Old Forge, Chartway Street, East Sutton, Maidstone, Kent ME17 3DW. *Bulbs*

E.W. King & Co Ltd., Monk's Farm, Kelvedon, Colchester, Essex CO5 9PG. *Flower seeds*

J. Parker Dutch Bulbs, 452 Chester Road, Manchester M16 9HL. *Bulbs (wholesale)*

Jacques Amand, The Nurseries, 145 Clamp Hill, Stanmore, Middlesex HA7 3JS. *Bulbs*

Kelways Ltd., Langport, Somerset TA10 9EZ. *Peonies and herbaceous plants*

Martin Davis Plants, Osric, 115 Calton Road, Gloucester GL1 5ES. *Lilies*

Mill Farm Plants and Gardens, Norwich Road, Mendlesham, Suffolk IP14 5NQ. *Pinks*

Peter Grayson, 34 Glenthorne Close, Brampton, Chesterfield, Derbyshire S40 3AR. *Sweet peas*

Pounsley Plants, Poundsley Coombe, Spriddlestone, Brixton, Plymouth, Devon PL9 0DW. *Tritonia; Crinum*

R.V. Roger Ltd., The Nurseries, Malton Road, Pickering, North Yorkshire YO18 7HG. *South African bulbs*

Sampford Shrubs, Sampford Peverell, Tiverton, Devon EX16 7EN. *Helenium and herbaceous plants*

Springbank Nurseries, Winford Road, Newchurch, Sandown, Isle of Wight PO36 0JX. *Nerine*

The Great Western Gladiolus Nursery, Moor's Edge, Athelney, Bridgwater, Somerset TA7 0SE. *Gladiolus*

FRUIT

Duchy of Cornwall Nursery, Cott Road, Lostwithiel, Cornwall PL22 0HW.
  Apples

Endsleigh Gardens, Milton Abbot, Tavistock, Devon PL19 0PG. *Top fruit*

Global Orange Groves UK, Horton Road, Horton Heath, Wimborne, Dorset
  BH21 7JN. *Citrus fruits*

J. Tweedie Fruit Trees, Maryfield Road Nursery, nr Terregles, Dumfries,
  Scotland DG2 9TH. *Strawberries and rhubarb*

Keepers Nursery, Gallants Court, Gallants Lane, East Farleigh, Maidstone,
  Kent ME15 0LE. *Top fruit*

R.V. Roger Ltd. (see above). *Soft fruit, especially gooseberries*

Reads Nursery, Hales Hall, Loddon, Norfolk NR14 6QW. *Figs, grapes and citrus
  fruits*

Thornhayes Nursery, St Andrews Wood, Dulford, Cullompton, Devon EX15
  2DF. *Top fruit*

TOMATOES, AUBERGINES, CAPSICUMS, CUCURBITS, ETC

Chase Organics (see above)

E.W. King (see above)

Edwin Tucker & Sons, Brewery Meadow, Stonepark, Ashburton, Newton
  Abbot, Devon TQ13 7DG

Seeds of Distinction, Abacus House, Station Yard, Needham Market, Suffolk IP6
  8AS

Simpson's Seeds, The Walled Garden, Horningsham, Warminster, Wiltshire
  BA12 7NQ

Thomas Etty Esquire, 45 Forde Avenue, Bromley, Kent BR1 3EU

Totally Tomatoes, PO Box 296, Torquay TQ2 5WB

ACKNOWLEDGEMENTS

The writing of this book has often meant dragging up pieces of information, almost forgotten, from layer upon layer of a hidden and half-remembered reservoir of experience – the depths of which have not been plumbed for a long time! This reservoir has been accumulating over a period of 50 years or so, during which time I have been involved continually in practising the art and science of horticulture as a professional.

A full-time life in horticulture has involved me in many facets of the profession, both practical and academic. The foundation from which this knowledge and experience was able to develop was provided by the opportunities afforded to me in the early days of my career. I was privileged to have worked with a succession of mentors who fostered my interests and allowed me unfettered rein (probably against their better judgement) to indulge my ideas. Among these, especially, were my Prof, J.P. Hudson of the University of Nottingham; F.W. Hankinson and John Pollard of the Surrey Farm Institute at Merrist Wood, where I took my first tentative professional steps; Eric Cordell of Hadlow College, and E.F.R. Stearn of Brooksby College, both of whom allowed me facility, authority and opportunity to develop and test ideas – to all of them I acknowledge my indebtedness for allowing me freedom of thought, and for encouraging my interests. With this group I must include my constant colleague and friend of those early years, Peter Hutchinson, who contributed many ideas and provided the support and comradeship which is an essential feature of progress and success (no man is an island …). I miss him still.

Heligan has provided an unparalleled opportunity, fairly late on in this chronology, for me to indulge in yet a further interest, which has also become virtually another passion.

The success of this venture, The Lost Gardens of Heligan, is down to one man, Tim Smit, but he will be the first to admit that it was a team effort, and among that team of people the contributions and efforts of John Nelson, Peter Stafford and Candy Smit, at significant periods, cannot be underestimated and cannot go by unheralded, and I add my acknowledgement.

All of the gardening staffs, right from the beginnings, have been core to the success. It would be invidious of me to pick out any one individual in particular,

as all have, in some measure, made an impact and have added to that tapestry of experience which has become The Lost Gardens of Heligan.

Although one can derive much knowledge from the wide variety of information sources, it is the personal interaction with others who have similar interests which allows the full development of ideas and practices. Over the last 15 years or so I would have been the poorer but for the discussions I have had with my friend and colleague Peter Thoday. We were also fortunate to collaborate, with Tim, on the formulation and establishment of the Eden Project. Peter Thoday has added immeasurably to my appreciation and understanding of a wide variety of issues, and I am privileged that he agreed to write the Foreword to this book.

The production of *Heligan: Fruit, Flowers and Herbs* (and all the modern technicalities this involves) has been in the capable and experienced hands of the publisher Alison Hodge, but it is because of the industry and effort of Candy Smit that all the text and the pictures have been put together and delivered on time. Compared with the efforts of both of them, simply writing the text has been a piece of cake!

This book depends for its impact as much on the photography as it does on the words. Foremost among the photographers has been the indefatigable Charles Francis. He has always been on hand to record an event or catch a plant at its best, often having to identify and photograph a plant without a detailed context! The proximity of his home within Heligan allows us to call on him at very short notice.

I cannot complete any catalogue of acknowledgement without paying tribute to my long-suffering family, who over the years have shown great forbearance and fortitude in putting up with my foibles: to my wife Helen and my daughters Harriet and Caroline – a sincere and big 'Thank-you'.

White cosmos, with cleome, clarkia and yellow rudbeckia, in front of the Peach House at Heligan

PICTURE
ACKNOWLEDGEMENTS

All photographs were taken at Heligan. Without these beautiful contributions, this book would have been impossible. They are the work of the following:

CHARLES FRANCIS: pages 2, 14 (top and bottom), 15 (top), 16 (bottom), 18 (bottom), 19 (bottom), 23 (top and bottom), 28 (top), 30, 37, 43 (top), 44, 45, 46 (top), 49, 51 (top and bottom), 54, 55, 56, 57, 61 (top and bottom), 62, 63, 65, 74 (top left, mid left and right, bottom right), 76 (top and bottom), 81, 85, 86, 87 (left and top right), 91, 92 (bottom), 93 (top), 94, 96, 97 (top, mid and bottom), 99 (top), 101, 103, 105 (bottom), 108, 109, 114, 115, 117, 118–19, 121, 122 (top and bottom), 123, 125 (top and bottom), 128 (top), 131 (top), 139, 145, 149, 150, 151, 156–7, 160, 162 (top and bottom), 164 (top and mid), 167, 169, 170 (top and bottom), 172, 174, 175, 177, 178, 180, 181 (top), 182 (all four), 185 (all except mid right), 186, 189, 190 (mid and bottom), 191 (top and bottom), 195, 199, 204 (top), 205 (top and bottom), 206 (bottom), 208, 209 (all four), 210, 215, 216 (top, mid and bottom), 217 (top and bottom), 218 (all), 219, 223, 225, 239, 240

DAVID HASTILOW: pages 7, 11, 12 (top and bottom), 13, 26–7, 29 (top), 31 (top), 32 (top), 35, 40, 92 (top and mid), 93 (bottom), 100, 104, 105 (top), 106, 120 (bottom), 124, 127 (top and bottom right), 130 (top), 131 (bottom), 132, 133, 138, 141, 143, 155, 159, 165, 179, 194, 200 (top), 208, 212, 229, 234, 236

COLIN HOWLETT: pages 120 (mid), 130 (bottom), 163, 221 (left)

ANDREA JONES LOCATION PHOTOGRAPHY: pages 7, 34, 41 (bottom), 78–9, 113, 200 (bottom), 211 (top and bottom), 222 (bottom), 226–7, 228 (all)

RICHARD KALINA: page 41 (top)

HERBIE KNOTT: pages 31 (bottom), 128 (bottom), 220 (top)

ANDREW PEARCE, FOTOGENIX: page 146

DAWN RUNNALS: pages 4, 15 (bottom), 16 (top), 18 (top), 22, 33, 36 (top and bottom), 39, 43 (bottom), 46 (bottom), 52, 59, 73, 74 (top right and bottom left), 75, 80, 87 (bottom right), 99 (bottom), 129 (bottom), 135, 136, 171, 204 (bottom), 207, 220 (bottom), 221 (right)

CANDY SMIT: pages 25, 28 (mid), 29 (bottom)

JULIAN STEPHENS: pages 89, 137, 152, 222 (top), 224

CLAIRE TRAVERS: pages 19 (top), 127 (bottom left), 142, 147, 164 (bottom), 181 (mid and bottom), 185 (mid right), 190 (top), 192, 196, 203, 206 (top)

SUE PRING: pages 24, 28 (bottom), 32 (bottom)

The following images are reproduced courtesy of: Commission Air, page 21; John Chamberlain, pages 128 (mid) and 129 (top); North Devon County Record Office, page 15 (top); Penelope Willis, page 120 (top).

We have made every effort to trace the owners of archival material, and trust all credits are correct.

First published in 2005 by
Alison Hodge, Bosulval, Newmill,
Penzance, Cornwall TR20 8XA, UK
www.alison-hodge.co.uk
info@alison-hodge.co.uk

© Philip McMillan Browse, 2005

The right of Philip McMillan Browse to be identified as the
author of this work has been asserted by him in accordance
with the Copyright, Designs and Patents Act 1988.

All rights reserved. No part of this work may be reproduced,
stored in a retrieval system, or transmitted in any form or by
any means, electronic, mechanical, photocopying, recording,
or otherwise without the prior permission of the publishers.

ISBN-13 978-0-906720-40-0
ISBN-10 0-906720-40-0

British Library Cataloguing-in-Publication Data
A catalogue record for this book is available from the
British Library.

Editor: Edward Cheese
Cover design: Christopher Laughton
Design and origination:
BDP – Book Design and Production, Penzance, Cornwall

Printed and bound in Singapore.